STEAM AT
THURSFORD

STEAM AT THURSFORD

George Cushing
with
Ian Starsmore

DAVID & CHARLES
Newton Abbot   London   North Pomfret (Vt)

02837204   482003441

ACKNOWLEDGEMENTS

With thanks from George Cushing to: Billy Barber, Charlie Barnard, Albert Bequart and family, Tim Blythe, Harry Bushell, Victor Chiappa, The Cole family, Dennis Cook, Reginald Dixon, Dr Green, Ralph Howden-Aspland, Bob Ince, Bill Jeans, Dick Joice, Derek Londrigan, Herbert Minns, Hank Möhlmann, Charlie Presland, Charlie Thurston, Walter Underwood, Sidney Utting, and a special thanks to the rest of the Cushing family for their support in sharing their lives with engines and organs.

YT	YP	YK	YF 4/82	
YN	YC	YW	YG	ML

British Library Cataloguing in Publication Data

Cushing, George
    Steam at Thursford.
    1. Cushing, George
    I. Title II. Starsmore, Ian
    791'1'0924   GV1811.C/

    ISBN 0–7153–8154–7

Filmset in Monophoto Baskerville
by Latimer Trend & Company Ltd, Plymouth
and printed in Great Britain
by Ebenezer Baylis & Son Ltd, Worcester
for David & Charles (Publishers) Limited
Brunel House   Newton Abbot   Devon

Published in the United States of America
by David & Charles Inc
North Pomfret   Vermont 05053   USA

CONTENTS

'All my life I've been used to picking
up a bent nail and straightening it.
Nowadays they chuck away the straight ones.'

GEORGE CUSHING Road mender and Collector.

INTRODUCTION

George Cushing has spent a working life of over fifty years repairing roads and doing haulage trips with steam engines and lorries in the countryside around the tiny village of Thursford, 9 miles from the north Norfolk coast. This would be an interesting enough, though ordinary, story in itself, but George also had a passion for fairs and made a collection of showman's engines, traction engines, organs and fairground art, which is without doubt one of the best of its kind in the world, and is exhibited in the village where he worked every day. The collection has evolved into a full museum, now open daily from Easter weekend until 31 October, and each year over 150,000 people make the journey down the road which winds off the main King's Lynn to Cromer highway, and leads to Thursford.

The place has become famous through newspapers and magazines, and the coach drivers certainly know the way. George didn't want to move to the city, and just made the barn bigger every time he needed more space. Taking the A148 from Lynn, there is a left turn a few miles before Holt, at a pub called the Crawfish. A short distance up this by-road is a farm, and further on, another left turn, now clearly signposted. For many years until about eighteen months ago, there was only one slender and badly leaning wooden signpost there. George has never believed in publicity. Written upon the post were the words 'To the Organs'. The lettering was small by advertising standards, imprecise and could easily have been missed by anyone who did not know for certain of its existence and exact whereabouts. Nevertheless that sign directed thousands of people over the years down a long, narrow, sweeping road from which there is a view of the Norfolk landscape spread in a shallow bowl against gently rising distant hills. The barn isn't visible from the top of the road, and the scene hasn't changed in years. It is still a working landscape, with perhaps smoke pluming over a row of trees on the other side of the cornfields.

At the bottom of the hill there is now a car park, and beyond the far hedge is the barn which contains the engines. Once inside you will see what all the fuss is about. It is full of gleaming, freshly painted steam engines, any one of which is worth a visit. The cavernous space of the barn is punctuated by beams of light which bounce off brass rods, wheels, canopies, sculptured figures, dragons and pipes. Among the exhibits are steam engines of all kinds, barn engines, huge 30ft organs, the only 50ft steam switchback in England, and one of the biggest Wurlitzer cinema organs ever in Europe. What is more, everything works. The engines could be driven out at any time, there are regular concerts on the Wurlitzer, the organs belt out a good tune and the switchback roundabout is full every day in the season as it was on the travelling fairs of the 1880s and 'nineties.

Fairs have always brought people out of themselves and the switchback is still doing it now. It could so easily have been sold abroad or broken up into pieces to be bought separately by other collectors or museums. No doubt the organ would have played to a private owner, but the cars and the carved work would have been labelled and exhibited silently with big 'DO NOT TOUCH' notices nearby.

The switchback is the most obvious sign that Thursford is a working museum and not a huddle of dusty exhibits. It is more a rip-roaring seaside call to come and have a go, get on the ride, plunge into the dips, up the hills, wave to your pals and have a good time. You see small children with their fingers pressed tightly round the carvings, staring into the dragons' faces or laughing at the wooden bandmaster on the organ as he moves his head sideways in time with the sound of the music. Older people are there too, and get caught up in the atmosphere. The museum is a show, and when the lights go on and the music starts, everyone seems drawn to it. The ride is often packed with pensioners, teenagers and children all having the time of their lives. The hills are very high, and by the time the machine is trundling round, most people find, sometimes to their surprise, that they're having fun, and the place is usually filled with the sound of their excitement.

The organs have the same effect. They play one after the other in rotation, and since every one has a different sound no one quite knows what's coming up next. Most of them have built-in surprise effects which are always corny but always work, like the whistles, telephone bells or surf and thunder. The jerky changes of tempo and melody are like a roller-coaster ride, and the music is a breezy 'blow your cares away' sound, full of all kinds of memories which pop up to startle you. These are foot-tapping and compelling rhythms which few can resist, however sophisticated they may think they are. It's 'boy or girl of your dreams' stuff, fairgrounds and romance, and it's been like that ever since George brought the first organ there.

When I told some friends that I was working with George on a book they looked puzzled and asked if he ever said much. They had only ever seen him as the man who started the organs, appeared from the back sometimes and drove the roundabout from the centre. His hands are usually filled with a spanner, lever or starter and his face has the air of a preoccupied mechanic. He has let the exhibits be the show and kept himself out of the limelight. He has never cared for appearance, likes to see people enjoying themselves and things working as they should, so he drives the switchback, listens to the sounds and watches.

This book is about George, and how the museum came to grow from the life he led, from the dreams and memories he had. The chapters which follow are based on recordings I made of him talking in the summers of 1979 and 1980.

I know that he would deny any talk of success. He is a working man who has managed by hard work and wit to become extremely wealthy, owning farms, a large laundry, land, buildings, and this extraordinary museum, but his wealth is not the most important or even the most noticeable thing about him. I am sure that he hasn't changed a bit since the age of twenty. He speaks rapidly with a strong Norfolk accent, won't tolerate fools or hangers-on, but he'll spend hours talking with anyone who is genuinely interested in fairs and engines, or has a feeling for them. He's often unshaven, dresses in old boots, worn trousers, check jacket and a cap which scarcely, if ever, leaves his head. His eyes are bright with humour and curiosity, and

9

I'm sure that he views the world with friendly and amused scepticism.

He told me recently of a fashion parade which was held at the museum, how everyone was dressed in expensive clothes of which he knew the exact price, and how he was wearing a good Harris Tweed which he had bought for a fiver in a rummage sale. It wasn't a pose that he was adopting, nor was he scoring points, it's just that he can't change his ways for anyone or anything and it wouldn't cross his mind to try and impress anyone. In his world the priorities are the care of the land and the implements which work upon it. These things need looking after, and whether they are hedges or steam engines they are things which last, and which represent real wealth.

As you will see from the story, George has always been involved with engines and fairs from early childhood, and most important, he has collected the things which he used to make his living. His working life was spent largely as a contractor, making roads for the local councils, mostly using steam engines. When steam became obsolete George kept his engines because they had served him well and because he loved them. He is, I am sure, the only major collector who used the engines in this way, and knows how hard they are to work. Once, not so long ago, steam engines were considered to be dirty, clumsy monsters which destroyed the ground on the village green, held up traffic and were generally inefficient. Whilst everyone else was apparently thinking something like that, and engines from all over the country were being broken up, George was buying them, keeping them and refusing to let go of the past. The steam age never ended for him. There was a continuity of using and collecting, and he was more correct in his judgement than those who let everything go.

As I was leaving after one of my visits earlier last year, he was still talking as he always did, right up to the last moment when I finally had to go. He was laughing and saying that he'd read somewhere that the ordinary traction engine was now a better status symbol than a Rolls-Royce. 'You could go from here to King's Lynn and perhaps see three or four Rolls, but you won't see an old engine. Those old millionaires have to have one of them now.' I think he enjoyed the joke.

He was born in 1904, to a poor family in Thursford. He was too young to fight in the First World War but worked on the land. His memories of childhood are very strong and in many ways are the real source of his passion for fairgrounds. He remembers his early life clearly and simply, and recalls most vividly his first visits to the fair at the nearby village of Walsingham. After working on the farms, George was third man in a steam engine team making roads. By the age of nineteen he was an engine driver himself, one of the youngest in the district, when drivers were considered to be men of importance and skill. He saved to buy his own engine out of a meagre wage, though he had to fight for it, and became the only private contractor in the area. He worked hard and did well mainly because he could be relied upon to undertake and complete the jobs he was asked to do, in the time specified and for the agreed price. He did tarmacadaming, carted road materials, corn and sugarbeet.

As well as being the youngest driver he was also one of the most skilful in the Norfolk area throughout the 1930s. In the 'forties and 'fifties he was collecting engines, and in the 'sixties he began to look again for the organs he had heard as a child. When he rescued the engines in the early years, they were worth only their value as scrap metal. He didn't know any more than anyone else that prices would increase, and bought them not as an investment but because he couldn't bear to see them destroyed. Now the collection is priceless and unique. The four Burrell engines which drove the rides and shows for the Thurston family are worth a fortune in themselves. Yet if their value was less than £40 now, I am sure that George would still think of them in the same way.

I first came to know him ten years ago. The museum was smaller then, the switchback wasn't yet there, and the yard was littered with engines through which weeds grew wild and thick. Some of the engines seemed to have taken root, inside the building pieces were scattered everywhere, and the bare hulks of engines being cleaned loomed in the recesses. I don't think that the collection was open every day, but when it was, and sometimes when it wasn't, the coach-loads would arrive and George would sprint from one organ to the next, pulling the switches which made each machine spring into life. He was in a world of his own, but unlike most people who live in a world of their own making, George managed to turn his into a more substantial one than the real and pragmatic existence around him. When he was told that the engines were worthless George didn't mind but carried on with the work he loved.

He dislikes leaving his home ground intensely, but he has made journeys that were extraordinary for someone of his temperament, going by traction engine to London, by jet to France or Belgium, and always in search of some piece of equipment about which he had heard. He always seemed to have had an ear to the ground, to his own private information service which was usually made up of people he had befriended by chance, who knew what he was after, and knew he could be trusted. I am sure that Percy Cole only brought the switchback to Thursford because he knew that it would be as safe with George as it would have been in his own hands. No doubt others would have made higher bids, and there were plenty of collectors who were after it. Good showmen are obsessive about the condition of their rides, and here was one which was unique on travelling fairs. George would not have had the ride if the Coles had not had confidence in him.

He loves the oil, the dirt and the smell of the engines, and enjoys the workings of the switchback as much as any showman. He works with the men he employs, like Billy Jeans, Bob Ince or Harry Bushell, and thinks nothing more of himself than that he is a man who has used his own hands to make a living. For all his wealth he has remained exactly the same person who began his professional life as an engine driver over fifty years ago. Those kinds of claims are often made of many people, but I can think of no one of whom it is more true. To go back into his life even further, I have a strong impression that the memories of Walsingham Fair from his early childhood are of an almost religious intensity. That surely sounds like an exaggeration, but imagine for a moment the Norfolk landscape as it was then, often bleak for the separated villages and above all, dark. The fairs brought electricity when there were at best gas-lit streets in the towns. They brought fantastic animals, dragons and peacocks, instead of farmyard animals. Even the horses and pigs on the roundabouts were more glamorous and powerful than life. George says himself that they were the only spectacle available. The memory of that first sight of the fair at Walsingham stayed with him. It was better than television or cinema and he made it more tangible.

The walls of his cottage where we talked for so many hours were filled with Dresden china figures like the large wooden figures on the organs. I can see him now looking into the pages of old photographs of Marenghis and counting the angels on the fronts. They seemed very real to him and I half think that he was in love with them: 'There's another and another. They're so lifelike . . . Wings. . . .' It wasn't until quite late in the interviews that I realised that his work could better be described as conservation rather than preservation. It was an act of conservation on his part to buy the engines in the 'forties. As far as George is concerned these were and still are working machines with useful life in them, and although he has always talked about the value of nostalgia, I always felt that he was making good his part of the world, restoring and replanting it as best he could. He talks about his work on the land in Chapter 3 and you will see that he was planting trees for the sake of the land long before ecology became a fashionable word. Whatever the season when I went to see him he always noticed which birds had arrived or had left, how abundant or scarce the insects or plants were, and he knew the importance of these things. He would run out in mid sentence because someone wasn't cutting a hedge properly. He knew exactly which trees could be cut back and which would be harmed, and he was distressed when other people didn't seem to know.

He has a very strong character, he is very shrewd, but he has also a great innocence which gives him the power to see the organs and engines as the spectacular wonders he had seen as a child. More educated people might have found them kitsch, grotesque or laughable; for many years the fashions in art and engineering didn't allow for Victorian or Edwardian extravagance and elaborate ornament. Things have changed now, largely due to the work of people like George. He is an original who has remained true to his own vision. Most of the contents of that barn which now amaze so many visitors from all over the world would have been dismantled, destroyed or would simply have rusted away without him.

He saw the last of an almost feudal England, faithfully remembers the details, and has continued to follow the old ways consistently against a background of the most rapid historical and technological changes. The cover of his family bible shows that for generations the Cushings have been farm labourers in Thursford, and he seems to have absorbed the wisdom of those people who have worked the

13

land so that it is part of him. He is one of the most simple and straight-forward of men, with a seemingly photographic memory of even the very early days of his own life in the village before and during the First World War. I felt that I could see the people he was describing, the postman cycling into the village every day, Fred Bushell driving the steam engine out to work, and George with his school mates sitting on the back of the cart as it trundled along to the fields. Work and pleasure ran together for them, and couldn't often be told apart.

He remembers the incidents of the villagers' lives, the food they ate, the games they played, the soldiers training in the fields in 1915, the funeral processions in the streets, the sounds of work from across the landscape, and the railways. Through everything in the picture he gave me, shone the image of the dragons and lights of the steam fairs, an emblem of all he felt for an older way of life. The plainness of his own appearance contrasts sharply with the drama and depth of his feelings for the old fairgrounds and the things he has saved at Thursford. Steam fairs were the brightest and most splendid of sights in East Anglia up to the 1930s, and no one knew them so well or can describe them better than George Cushing. What follows is simply a record of his memories as he told them to me himself, with true Norfolk genius.

Ian Starsmore
January 1981

CHAPTER I

HARVEST FAIR

Sometimes the oddest things come unbidden into your mind to unlock the other memories. I remember the green landscape and the steam sounds from early on, and being very small, and having a country boy's knife. I don't know who gave it to me, but it shone like silver and I lost it. I had gone with some friends down to a pond near my house, and on the way back we stopped to play on some straw. It seems to me that the knife came out of my pocket, and I can still see us in my mind's eye, turning over the straw in that summer field in 1907 to look for it. It was like the story of the needle in the haystack, and I never did find it, probably because I was much too young. It was long before I went to school, which meant nothing like as much to me as the knife or the fields, either then or in memory now.

I didn't like the discipline that school asked of us, standing in the corner, books on our heads. I didn't like the writing of lines or the way that time seemed to stretch as 4 o'clock approached. I hadn't wanted to go there from the first. My mother had to drag me by the arm, and when it was over I raced out to the fields. I was much more interested in the life of the village, and couldn't wait to get out there.

Thursford was a small isolated place of about two hundred people, a hall, a church, a pub and a few houses, yet it was a complete world for children and adults alike. The figures and activities of those who worked there filled my mind so that I remember them as clearly as though it were yesterday that I had seen them. Life was simpler, more individual, and slower. We felt the great events of the world as we would the ripples on the edge of a pond, and for a few years things were perfect for the growing boy I was.

There were very rarely any changes in the pattern of daily routine. There weren't even many bicycles about, and I remember talking to an old man in nearby Holt many years later, who told me that the furthest he had been in his life was 6 miles away to the harbour at Blakeney. You could go 15 miles inland into Norfolk and meet people who had never seen the sea. Some of the villages were miles away from the nearest railway station, and since there was no other way to make a journey of any length, it was important to us that we had our own station in Thursford.

I remember waiting for the postman with some school friends. There was no post office in the village itself, so that when he came he was one of the events of the day for us. He was a link with the world beyond the boundary of the main road, and when most of the men in the village walked to work, he came on a bicycle painted official post-office red. We called him 'Bob the Postman' in an obvious way, but also because his uniform and bike seemed to form his identity. His real and full name was Robert Tipple, and he would come from Guist in the morning, stay all day to go round the village, and then go away at night with the post he had collected. The post village of Guist was about 7 miles away from Thursford, so he had quite a journey to make each day. Later, after the First War, the post came from Walsingham and Postman Parker came twice a day on his bike, morning and afternoon. There never was much post to collect from the box, even though it was only a halfpenny to send anything, so the postman's job was more relaxed, and he had time to get to know everyone. He had a long way to bike of course, but the deliveries were fewer, and since most of us were on foot, the post office bike seemed very grand and efficient. Not all postmen had the luxury of a bicycle, and there were many villages who had 'Walking Postmen'. There was one in Fakenham who had to deliver post to Ryburgh for many years before the war. I remember watching Bob's uniformed figure make his rounds, and my mother told me that I used to stand near the door to see him coming long before I could talk properly and shout out 'Bob the Postman' if he came to our gate.

A family called Bushell had threshing machines in the village, and that's probably where I got my interest in steam engines. We were surrounded by them and the railways. The Bushells lived in the centre of the village and I was friendly with them all, especially Joe who was a lad of about my own age. They had three threshing machines which would be out at different places and most of the men used to walk out to the farms to their work. I've heard Harry Bushell say that he's known a man walk 5 or 6 miles three times a week to do one day's work, because when he arrived at the farm it was too wet or windy to thresh. That was something that very often happened.

My grandfather on my mother's side, two of her brothers and my father made a living by cutting drains for the fields. All of the work was done by hand then, and they had to walk terrific distances, from Great Snoring to Raynham or Stiffkey which was about 9 miles. In fact they had to cover everywhere within a 10-mile radius of Great Snoring where they lived. There were drains everywhere; they were an important part of country life, especially near the rivers, because they always needed to be cleared of debris. The grandfather and the brothers continued digging drains for a living all their lives, and never did do anything else. They used to charge so much to clear a chain length of ditch, depending on the difficulty of the work and how big or wide the drains were. I used to go with them often. I used to stay with my grandmother at Great Snoring in the Christmas holidays, and would walk to Barsham from there, about $2\frac{1}{2}$ miles away to take my uncles' dinner or bottle of drink. Then I'd spend the rest of the day with them, and come home in the evening. They had a little pony and cart, and a ride in that was something.

I can't remember any newspapers being delivered in Thursford until the First War. An old village man named Jack Oakes used to go around with them, and often they would arrive late because they had come into the station on the midday passenger train instead of the earlier one at 9.00am. Then old Jack would swear and create, because he had the whole round to do in an afternoon, delivering the lot at a halfpenny each, and rush about to get home by dark. I don't know whether he always managed it, but he always made a fuss if he was late. Thursford is a village which is spread out over 2 miles or so, so that although Jack only had a few deliveries, he had a long way to go to make them. It's a mile up to the workhouse, and another mile to the station from the village and a good way out on the main road to Brookhill Farm. Also most of the houses aren't right on the edge of the road. If you go through Thursford you will see that they are well set back with a long pathway to them, unlike Barney where they are all in a row up to the road, so Jack couldn't just throw the papers in the letterboxes. Thursford was and still is a village scattered about, as Jack would testify.

I didn't see many motor cars during the First War, although there were a few. There were a lot of soldiers about, especially up to 1916, and they were all on horseback. The Buckinghamshire Yeomanry were stationed at Great Snoring and we boys used to go to see them there. There would be masses of them come past in wagons and with horses, so that when we went down the main road on a Saturday we could nearly always bet on seeing them, and I never saw a single petrol-driven vehicle with them during the whole of the war, which surprises me now.

The first motor car that I saw belonged to a farmer named Crayford who came from Houghton, and that would have been in the early part of the war. Dr Steward used to come from Walsingham in an old model T Ford. Dr Fisher from Fakenham had one too, and so did the parson from Hindringham. He had married a brewer's daughter, and so he could afford to have a motor. Once I remember he gave us a lift. We were all in the scouts before 1916, and we used to walk to the scout troup at Hindringham two or three nights a week, and once or twice to Walsingham. Perone, the parson, took us there one Saturday in his car, and we thought that was marvellous. Cars didn't have electric lights, they had acetylene lamps and oil lamps on the front, but as we bumped along the road in the gloom, we felt like lords.

We didn't see the first buses on solid rubber tyres until well after 1918, and the first bus service from Fakenham to Norwich started in the late 1920s, though by that time I had been to London and seen the old solid-tyred, open-topped buses there. I first went in 1923 to stay with an aunt of mine, and I remember being impressed by the buses I saw, and wondering how the driver coped, sitting in the open as he did.

In the separateness of the village, the church was an important meeting place. Most people went on Sundays, two or three times, and all the children went to the Sunday School. There were a lot of us in the village then. I remember eighty on the school register, and Harry Bushell who is older than me says he remembers ninety-three children on the roll call. Thursford Church was full every week with all the people from the hall—the servants, the butlers, the coachmen and all the Scott-Chads themselves who owned the hall. There was a crowd, and for special occasions like Harvest Festival you could hardly move as we all squashed into the church. Every seat would be full, and you'd have to stand to get in there.

I was in the choir for a long time, like most of the boys and girls in the village. We had gowns and surplices like the parson, and enjoyed dressing up to march down the centre of the church. The organ would play, and our procession would go past the crowded pews, led by the smallest of the boys, with the parson following as the last one. The girls were always there already in their stalls. We were lucky then in Thursford because Christmas was much considered. It was more of a religious thing than it seems now, and we shared it together. Also it was the only time of year that we had a cheap toy or saw such things as oranges or nuts. We used to hang our stockings up, and be thrilled with the smallest of gifts. What we really looked forward to was the party given every year by the Scott-Chads for the children. They owned most of the village and they gave us a high tea in the school, after which we sang carols and played games until long after we would have been in bed on an ordinary day. At the end of the evening we all went to the huge Christmas tree at the end of the room, where there was a present for every boy and girl in the village. All the chairs and tables would be stacked at one end of the room for the games, and the tree would be left glowing with candle-light. The servants who had been sent from the hall to wait upon us would stand to watch us open our presents, to see our excitement. Everything on the tree was of the same value, so that no child would feel that he had something less than anyone else. There was a similar party for us given at the hall itself in the summer, when we had long tables set out in the courtyard there for the tea which the servants brought to us, and swings, see-saws and fun and games for all of us.

Throughout the year we made our own amusements. I think that it was the same all over England, with the games following the seasons, even though there were no means of communication. There was a skipping season, and a hopscotch season, we had spinning tops with string in April, and later we had hoops which we would send bowling down the lanes. At a certain time of the year we played buttons and marbles, and then in the autumn we made pop-guns from the acorns when they were fit. The gun was made out of a piece of elder, with the pith taken out of the middle, and we'd flatten the end of a nut stick, put the acorn in one end, the stick in the other, push the whole contraption into our stomachs and the acorn would come flying out of the other end with a pop, and travel for yards.

We had all sorts of games at school such as Fox and Hounds, and 'One Foot Over You Must Go', in which we made a mark on the road, and another a hundred yards from it. There would be a lot of boys in between the marks, and one boy would have to run the gauntlet starting at one end to try and reach the other without being caught. Once your foot was over the first line you had to run, and if you were caught you had to join the catchers. We were never at a loss to know what to do. If we weren't chasing each other up the road, we would be running the hoops, climbing or inventing new games. Nowadays most schools have their own playing fields, or there is an emphasis on organised sport, such as football, tennis and hockey, but there were lots of games that we used to play in which two or three of us could get together in the evening and have fun. We didn't need a team, and in a small village such as Thursford with its scattered houses, this was an advantage, because any number could play, and it didn't matter who turned up or when.

Thursford Hall was fairly big, and there was a full staff including footmen, kitchen maids, butlers, chambermaids, and they even had their own bakery there. The north wing, which was the servants' quarters, is still in existence, and you can see it from the main King's Lynn to Cromer road. The main hall was pulled down after the First War, when the old lady Scott had died and the whole estate was split up, so we saw the last of a world which had gone on for hundreds of years.

I remember that the dinner gong from the hall was one of the three or four sounds by which we knew the time, because it went at the same hour every evening. Also we could hear the buzzer from the railway factory at Melton Constable, which went at 5 minutes to 8.00am and then again at 8.00am before the war. We could hear the sound for miles around, just as if it were up the road a few steps. Then there was the buzzer at Ryburgh, which was 7 miles away at the foundry, and the whistle from the printing works at Fakenham which we could often hear. Melton buzzer was the loudest because it was set up on a hill, and was very, very strong. There were five or six hundred men working there, drivers and firemen, and they too had to walk long distances to get there, sometimes 8 miles or more. I remember one man going through the village here in the evening and again the next morning on his way to Melton from Bartham, which is a distance of about 9 miles, a long way on foot. So, we had several things by which we could tell the time, and the bell on the tower at the hall used to ring at 7.00pm for dinner.

The estates of Thursford Hall date back to before the time of William the Conqueror. Obviously the building itself has been re-built several times since then, but the lands have been handed down from generation to generation since a man named Kettle lived there before the Conquest. Kettlestone village was owned by the last landlords to inhabit the hall, and we think that there must be a connection between the names. In the days of William the Conqueror, Thursford was called Tursford, after an unbridged ford here, and the hall was owned by a man by the name of Gothic. Over the years it came into the Guybon family, whose name you can still see on the vaults of the church. They lived here for a couple of hundred years, and several of them are buried here. The last of them died in the late seventeenth or early eighteenth century, and left the hall to George Chad, who was a recorder at King's Lynn. The hall stayed in the Chad family until about 1852, when the last one died at the age of twenty-one or so, and ownership was transferred to a niece called Rawlinson, who had married a man named Scott. One condition of their ownership was that they took the name of Chad, lived at Thursford and carried on the estate and the church. I've actually seen a copy of the will, and that is how the Scott-Chads came to live in the hall. Captain Scott-Chad was the last and he died, without children, after the Second War, leaving the Pinckley Hall Estate which had belonged to the Scott family intact, though of course Thursford Hall Estate had been sold years before.

I have a catalogue of the sale of Thursford Estates, and there are photographs of the complete hall, and the cottage where I live now, which was then the keeper's house, and was sold to the Andersons from whom I bought it later. I couldn't have bought it at the original sale, because I was being paid about 5 bob a week, and didn't have enough for a shooting jacket. You can get an idea of the size of the main building if you look at the pieces that are left standing. All the rest was pulled down, split up and sold, most of it going to America, including the panelling in the drawing room, the oak room, the staircase and the marble fireplace.

Like all the estates around here Thursford was a big employer, with men in the garden, bricklayers, carpenters and a saw mill. When it was sold it affected the whole economics of the village. The same kind of event went on in several villages around here. I recently saw a friend of mine who is a forester at Holkham Hall, for whom we have done a lot of work over the past twenty years on the 13-odd miles of road there. He told me that when he started he had eighteen men with him, and now only one, and there used to be twenty people employed in the 5 or 6 acre garden, where there aren't any now. Holkham used to have 100 farms and 600 houses, so you can just imagine how many were employed in keeping them all in repair. Now there is hardly anyone employed there, and the changes at Thursford happened as part of the same inevitable process. I miss the sight of the hall, and the continuity of life which it signified.

The railway was ever such an important part of my life. When I was about five years old I went missing from home one afternoon, and they eventually found me at about 9 o'clock at night near the railway station. My mother and father were looking for me along with everyone else, and were desperately wondering what had happened to me, and there I was looking at the trains.

In my school days I used to go there with the other boys on Saturday afternoons to see the trains go through, and later we went down there to watch the 8.17pm arrive. There'd be people coming off the train who had been to market, and the porters were there loading the milk churns to go on to London. In Thursford village itself we could hear the puffing of the old engines going up what we called Barney Bank about a mile away, where there was a gradient, and of course when they went down the bank they'd speed at about 60 miles an hour with a roaring and shaking.

I remember the first time we saw the gates open at the crossing. They were operated from the signal box, and there was no way for us to see how they worked. All at once the bell rang and the gates swung open, apparently by themselves, then we saw the signal go down about half a mile down the line, where again there was no one to be seen, and we all thought that it was magic. That may seem unbelievable now, but we only knew what we saw in our own village, mostly horses and carts, and to our childish minds the railway was remarkable.

The only way you could go out of your village was to go by train, and I think that the first journey I ever made was to Fakenham. There was all the excitement of waiting at the station, seeing the gates open, the train arrive, and then climbing into an empty compartment and chuffing along through the landscape, seeing from the train the places where I had stood to watch. Most adults felt the same excitement that we did, because the train was the only mechanical means of getting about. It was a very different experience from the horse or bike, and the train remained a marvel for many years. There's something about a steam engine that attracts people. On Sunday nights there'd be people from miles around come to the station. We couldn't get near the train for the men, women and children standing there, just looking at the engines. They hadn't a chance to see them in the week, because they were all at work, and they came in from all the villages like Hindringham and Binham to be there, thinking nothing of the 4-mile walk in the light of a summer evening. To be truthful there wasn't much else that you could do on a Sunday night, but we made a lot out of it, and found it rewarding.

Later on we used to go to Yarmouth on August Bank Holiday when there was a special excursion there. It ran every year from 1919 until 1939 as a regular thing, and it was ever so popular. Also there were the half-day trips to London, 6 bob return from Thursford, leaving here at 11.00am and coming back from London at 11.00 in the evening. I went on several of them, and the trains were packed. We caught the train to Lynn, then Peterborough, and straight through to King's Cross. The trains weren't so slow that you'd be on them very long, and the journey seemed quick.

Even today there are few machines that are as majestic as a railway engine all polished up and painted as they used to be. They stood there, then they'd start up with a chuffing and blowing, with the clouds of steam pouring from the chimney. There isn't much to see on a lorry even when the engine is at full throttle, but on a railway train you see the cranks and the wheels polished and moving, the smoke and the whistle, smell the heat in the air, and feel the vibration of the tracks through the ground beneath your feet.

When I was at school, our favourite night to visit the station was on Saturday. We were free then, and Monday seemed a long way away. We had done all our chores during the day so that we could meet there. That seems a little surprising too now, and I'd be afraid to let a boy of eight or nine walk a mile or so after dark to a railway station or anywhere. Yet we used to walk for miles and never imagine that anything could go amiss. I would walk to my grandmother's at Great Snoring when I was seven, and within a few years we all walked to Fakenham to get a 'pound of overweight', as we called it, for our mothers. This was an early version of margarine, and if you bought a pound you had a quarter free. We were so hard up that the least bit of money was important and the walk was worth it. There was a Brenner's Bazaar at Fakenham too, and Dereham, where the maximum cost of any one item was one penny, so they came to be known as the 'Penny Bazaars', just as Woolworth's was called 'The Sixpenny Store' when it first started. We walked everywhere, there was no traffic, and we knew everybody in the district, so we were safe. Anyway there was always a crowd to meet the trains, especially on the late Saturday, when people were returning from Norwich Market, and others had arrived in pony chaises and carts to take them home. The fare to Norwich and back was only twopence or threepence, and so everyone went, either for business or pleasure, and all the farms for 6 miles around Thursford sent out their carts to meet the homecoming families.

We used to go into the porter's room. He never seemed to mind, and there was a fire there in the winter time to keep us warm while we waited for the last passenger train to arrive. Every so often goods trains would go through and this gave us a lot of excitement. There were the empty trucks going down towards King's Lynn, and the loaded ones coming up the other way, not much faster than a walking pace because of the gradient. There were two extremes of speed, the loaded trains pulling up the hill, chuu-uff, chuu-uff . . . and we used to wind our arms in imitation of the wheels, and recite in unison 'Too many, Damn and Blast . . .' and think that we heard the engine say it with us. Then in the other direction the trains would come past like the wind, ruffling our hair and drowning our shouts with the noise and the rattling of the empty trucks, which you could hear for miles, especially on a still night.

As soon as we saw the gates open we knew that something would be happening and out we'd go, in gangs of two or three. We used to meet all sorts of other groups of kids from the other villages like Barney, and call out to them in the darkness surrounding the station. We spent hours there as schoolchildren, those of us who were interested.

Even after I had left school, and much later when I had been working for a number of years the affection for the railway stayed with me, and maybe helped me work for them with a bit of understanding of what was needed. I came to know all the signalmen in the Fakenham and Raynham areas, and when I was working away from home, living in the road van, I would go to spend an hour or two with them in the evenings. They didn't mind because they liked to have someone to talk with, even though it was against railway regulations. At night there were no officials about and anyway we did no harm. Charlie and George from Raynham and I spent many hours chatting through the night. You have to remember that there was nothing else to do but sit and read, and I was glad of the company. Things have changed now, you can get in a motor car and travel further after tea than my father went in all his life. But then the railway was so important to us in more ways than one. It helped us trade, brought us news from outside, took us on the only journeys possible to us and entertained all of us.

Railway engines were made and repaired at the works at Melton Constable only 4 miles from us in Thursford. In Great Snoring they made harvest elevators and threshing equipment, and in the Walsingham foundry they used to make ploughs and harvesting machines and drills to be exported all over the world via the railway, so there was plenty of activity in the district.

The roads were made from the stone in the local pits, and were flattened by steam roller. I can remember the roller that eventually came to be the first I bought, and which I still have now, arriving new to the council in 1913, and rolling past the school in 1914. It seems a funny thing now when I think that it was all those years ago. As a lad I used to go all over the place to see it working. Someone would come to tell us that there was a roller about, and we'd all be off like a flash, running to see it.

The roads were adequate for the traffic that was on them. One of my jobs as a boy was cow keeping on the road. The local farmer would turn his stock out to browse on the bank and the verge, to save the grass on the meadow. That shows you how little traffic there was on the roads. Naturally there had to be someone there to look after them in case they broke away, and that was my job. Each farmer would use the banks of the fields that he owned. Most of the roads weren't very wide and had large verges with all kinds of grass and hog-weed which the sheep, bullocks or cows loved.

In my mind now I can see us clearly rumbling along the road to Wells in a big wagon pulled by two horses. The Sunday School used to organise an outing once every year to Wells-next-the-Sea which was about 9 miles away. A farmer would lend the wagon, and all the children would sit on the wooden seats along the edges, with a couple of teachers to see we behaved ourselves. There was no rush to get to the sea. The horses never galloped, occasionally they'd trot, and mostly they would walk, but we thought it was great fun. Nine miles in a horse and wagon was the equivalent of going 70 or 80 in a motor car. We went through the villages to get to Wells, and it seemed much further than it was. It was a terrific event. Down on Wells beach, and all along the road which led to the beach were masses of horses and wagons from the other villages. The horses would be quite happy to stand there all day munching away with their feed bags until the time came to come home. We'd all played in the sands, splashed in the sea, met new friends and were tired out by then. The journey back was lovely, watching the light fade, seeing the animals watch us from the fields and woods. We sometimes managed to get back to Thursford by dark, but if we didn't we had an old lantern hanging on the front of the wagon to light our way home. We did that every year until the commencement of the war, from when I was about six years old until 1914. Though there weren't many trips, I remember them clearly.

The seaside was a different world. I went with my mother on August Bank Holidays too. We used to walk to Walsingham, 4 miles, then go by train from there, climbing on the Wells train at Walsingham station. We did that a few times, and I remember particularly

August 1914. When we came to the beach I played for a long while on the sand, and I was aware that all around me people were talking about whether there would be a war. I didn't know what a war was, but the air was heavy with conversation about it, and within a few days, on August 4th, the First World War began.

Oblivious to the real meaning of all that, we played on the beach, made castles, rivers and drew in the wet sand. We never had ice-cream or chips or anything like that. We couldn't have afforded to buy them anyway. We had bread and butter or cheese, and maybe a bottle of lemonade, because there were no flasks. There was a tea bar down there but I can't remember buying much out of it, because we had no money. We kept mostly to ourselves, playing with our mates from school and the village, being a bit suspicious of the foreigners from other places. Sometimes, when I was just with my own family, my sister and I would play with a boy and girl from another family, but that's all.

I remember the Coronation Sports at Thursford in 1911 on the park, to celebrate the crowning of King George. All the children from our village went to the feed which the Chads gave, and the adults had a dinner in what is now our corn barn. The same thing happened after the war in 1918 to welcome the peace. We were so much together with each other in our own village that we didn't need people from outside, or so we felt.

There was so much that we shared, from the trivial games of childhood and youth to the more serious things of adult life. We played truant from the school one year to watch the soldiers doing their training manoeuvres. There were a lot of them in 1915, and one morning they started to come through along the main road, three or four hundred of them with limbers, guns and weapons of all kinds. It was five or ten minutes to nine, and we stood to watch them so that by the time they had gone past, it was too late to go to school. This is what we told ourselves, and there weren't many in class that morning. The soldiers would come on other days from all directions, through the village or through the woods, and we'd run to the Crawfish pub or down the lane to get to where we could stand to see them. We often heard them coming from Fakenham with the iron wheels making a trundling noise on the hard granite roads. We ran to the Crawfish to see the convoy and count the soldiers or guns.

We regarded everything in the village as an attraction, for our amusement. The blacksmith's shop was right next to where we lived. The family's name was Ram, and there were two or three sons who were more or less the same age as me, with whom I had gone to school. The blacksmith worked until 8 o'clock at night and in the winter time that was somewhere we could go. They'd be hammering out horseshoes, and we used to like to pump the bellows if we could, until we were fed up with it, then we'd race out again into the dark.

In the summer we would go down to the beck. The River Stiffkey ran nearby and we went there to paddle or strip off to swim in the deep part. As soon as ever we came out of school we'd down our tea and be off to the river. We spent all our light nights in summer there, and most of the summer holidays. There were dozens of us, and I often thought how lucky we were to be able to swim and play there, within half a mile of our homes. We used to race the distance there and run our hoops as we went.

I often think of the old people who were in the village then, they were part of the daily scenery, like Mr Alan the Church Warden, with his donkey and cart. There were others I remember, and whose passing I regret. Funerals were events. When there was a death, the coffin had to be carried half a mile from the village to the church, and then again to the cemetery. There were always two boys holding stools, who walked next to the men carrying the coffin, so that when anyone wanted a rest the boys could put down the stools to support the coffin. The small procession would halt for a minute or two, and then away it would go again. There would be a terrific following and nearly all the village would turn out. The death of an individual affected the whole village and grief was shared. I remember three old ladies in particular, Mrs Goole, Mrs Gent, and Mrs Caley, standing around a grave crying for someone who was no relation of theirs at all. Funerals were different things altogether from the kind of things they are now, or so it seems to me. Everybody went out of respect. I carried the stools for about three years, and I remember carrying them for the funerals of Mrs Groom, poor old Dan Alan the warden, and several others. We were paid a shilling every time, which was a lot of money to us in the days of the penny bazaars. We were very sad, but that didn't stop us being boys.

Nothing that happened to any one of us was an isolated event.

What you have to remember is that these people in the village had lived there all their lives, and usually their fathers and mothers had been born there too, so that everyone was very close, and knew each other well. Hardly anyone worked away from the village, or even went out of the village at all. There were lots of people there who had never been more than 5 miles away all their lives. There was no point in going to the next village, because it was exactly the same as yours, and there was nothing to do when you got there.

We had a pub, the Crawfish I've mentioned, and we used to go down there on Saturday nights, though we weren't allowed in, because we weren't old enough. It was usually worth a visit after we'd been to the station, and all the people who had come from the train left their ponies and carts outside tethered to the wall. Inside would be full. They'd be singing all the old songs of the day and we'd wait outside listening with the ponies. That was the only night when we went there, because, though beer was only twopence a pint, there were few who could afford it more than once a week.

We made our enjoyment out of the day-to-day activities. There were two boys with whom I was friendly called Moy, and their father usually worked until 4.00pm on a Saturday, taking a load of corn to Ryburgh or Walsingham. We went with him for the ride on several occasions, with the wheat for the mills where they ground the flour. Joe Bushell and I would go with his father, helping behind the engine and trailers. When they weren't threshing they'd be doing haulage work of some kind, and we went with them to take gravel to Holt, Hindringham Old Hall, and two loads of bricks from the kilns at Barney to Wells where some new houses were being built.

If there was anyone threshing on a Saturday we'd be there too, catching the rats, and anyway it was an event for us to watch the threshing machine. When they moved away, perhaps on a Saturday afternoon we'd follow, and if it was to Kettlestone or Little Snoring a couple of miles away, we'd ride on the back of the old straw pitcher, then walk home afterwards. Briston Fair always finished on a Saturday night and moved to Walsingham on the Sunday, and when we heard the steam engine coming in the distance we'd run out to meet it, then follow behind it through the village. The vans were all pulled by horses, Mrs Dack would be driving the living

'A steam engine and a team of men cutting the fields with self-binders. The children in the village used to walk the length of the field putting the bound corn into stooks, or "shocks" as they were called in Thursford.'

wagon, and Harry Dack the organ truck. The only mechanical haulage was done by the traction engine pulling the centre truck and two other loads. We could all hear the fair on its way long before it arrived, and almost everyone in the village would come out to stand near the edge of the road and watch. It only happened once a year, and we waited for it each time with great excitement.

Wrights the Millers at Walsingham had a Foden Steam Wagon, which we used to call 'The Nipper', and it would come through Thursford on its way to deliver loads of flour to the bakeries at Melton and elsewhere. More often than not it would do a return trip through in the evening. When we heard it, someone would shout, 'Cor, are you going to meet the Nipper?', and before we knew it we were running after it right through the village as far as the workhouse. Once, after we had done that, we met Fred Bushell at the end of the village with his pony, off to take some lubricating oil to the engines out working, and Joe and I hopped on there, waved cheerio to the others and thought we were grand fellows. Sometimes we drove the loads on the farms later, and they trusted us to take out the horse and wagon stacked high with corn, which really was something.

The only visitors to the village were those who came there on business of some sort, perhaps to bring or sell food. There was an old baker called Charlie Coop who came round three times a week from Kettlestone, on Mondays, Wednesdays and Fridays. A fisherman, George Earl, came on Saturdays, and Bob Buck, the Cockle Man, came from Stiffkey twice a week shouting 'All Alive' at the top of his high-pitched voice that you could hear all over the village. At certain times of year he used to bring samphire, and was sold out as soon as he opened his mouth to call his wares. Nothing cost very much. There were cockles, winkles and mussels, and it was surprising how much of a feed we could get out of them. We used to have winkles for tea on Sunday, eating them with a pin, and it's a hell of a job to get them out, so that by the time we had pulled out eight or nine of them and eaten them with bread and butter we thought we'd had a huge meal. It was impossible to eat them quickly, twizzling the pin around to get them out, but anyway they were tasty. George Earl's bloaters were very good and cheap too, twenty for a shilling. What he didn't sell in the day he'd take down to the Crawfish to sell off, and he never took any home with him. Whatever fish were in season we had in plenty, and Jack Oak would bring round rabbits that he had caught at the warren to sell for a few coppers. So we didn't do so badly. I could go to the farm and buy a halfpenny's worth of skimmed milk, which was thick then because there were no mechanical separators, and we had as much butter and milk from there as we could afford. We had the fruit from our own trees, which was just as well since there was nowhere to buy it from, and nothing to buy it with either.

In the wintertime we would talk and read at home. Some villages had special reading rooms, where you could play draughts and dominoes as well, but Thursford wasn't big enough for that. There was usually an oil lamp inside and a lot of snow outside, but that didn't bother us because we only needed to go as far as the village boundary, walking about, and we had most of the things we wanted. I can't remember that we ever went without any essentials even when the village was cut off for days in the worst winters, when no one could get in or out. Once we sent a man across the fields on horseback to get bread for the rest of us, and we had to pour milk down the drain because there was no one to collect it from us. We were more or less self-sufficient for food and entertainment. My mother used to make her own bread, and usually had a stock of flour. We made our own beer and wine from the fruit we had collected in the year, so we never used to take any harm.

In my school days I had lived the kind of free and happy life that country boys had done for centuries, and it wasn't until I left school in 1916, when I was twelve, that I really encountered the harder side of work. Although the official leaving age was fourteen, during the First World War you could leave earlier if there was a job for you. Of course people were called up in their thousands, almost every able-bodied man went out to fight, and the slaughter was unimaginable. I didn't realise that at the time, but it was because of it that I went to work on the farm.

There were lots of jobs for young boys and all the work was done with the help of horses. For instance when the root crops were growing in the spring it was a boy's job to lead the horse pulling the hoe, which an older man would operate, and I wished I hadn't left school because we were really made to work. I remember leading the horse whilst we were hoeing mangolds and turnips. Well, a horse is a big thing to a twelve-year-old boy, and that old horse would sometimes jump from his front legs, jerk, snort and blow through his nose, and nearly pull my arm out of the socket. When we turned round at the end of the field the horse would rear up to bite some leaves off the hedge, whilst the old man was still trying to hoe. I can remember the man now shouting at me, 'Hold off, Hold off, can't you', in a long narrow 10-acre field. We were there from six in the morning to six in the evening, and I remember having high leather boots with hob-nails and a very sore heel; a damn great sore place on my heel as big as a two bob bit and I didn't know hardly how to walk. I was limping up and down this damn field. When I went home that night my mother washed my heel and bandaged it up because I had to go again the next day. You only took two ridges at a time and as you can imagine you were a long while doing 10 acres. I remember that much about it, very well.

In the winter time there were lots of cold jobs, and one of those which I used to do was going to get loads of white turnips to throw out to the cows and the bullocks on the meadow. You'd have to pull them up, without gloves, those frosted old turnips, get hold of them and pull them up to throw them on to the cart. Every now and again your hands would be frozen cold, you'd get the hot aches, and I remember crying and having cold and wet feet. At twelve years old you weren't too old to cry. You see there were no such things as rubber boots, wellingtons or water boots for us. You had 'buskins' if you could afford them, and 'buskins' go round your boots at the ankle, like gaiters, but if you went in mud any higher than that, the water ran in over the tops of your boots. So you had wet and cold feet, cold hands, and then your mind went back to your school days. After the first few weeks I wished I was back behind a desk, but there was no returning.

There was always work to be done. In harvest time you'd be raking across the fields following behind the men as they pitched. Some farms had a rake pulled by a horse, but on our farm we had to do it ourselves. Then of course we used to go acorn picking when they were in season, and farmers would pay us a few coppers, because they used to feed acorns to the pigs. There were times when we went stone picking. Some of the fields had a lot of stones on them and clearing them was a job that was often given to boys and women, because they would do it cheaply. A boy was glad to go and earn a penny or two and so was a woman. Lots of those jobs were done on Saturdays or evenings when it was light in spring.

The country roads that are now tarmacked and tarred had grass growing in the middle. The only traffic that was on them was horse traffic from the farms. In most areas of Norfolk, and in this area in particular, fields were very small compared with the size they are now. They were only 6 acres or 10 acres, and they all had their various names, 'The Bush Close', 'Tun Croft'; there were lots of different names and every field had one. Some were called simply 'The Eleven Acres' or 'The Eight Acres'. The village life was all we knew, people hardly went out of the village they were born in. They went as far as they could walk which wasn't a great distance, although they walked a lot further than they do now. It was thought nothing to walk to Fakenham which was 5 miles away, or anything up to

33

10 miles. Along the roads there were hedges all round the fields, then there were trees on the meadows which the animals would go under in the summer. I suppose they got a little breeze there although wherever they went the flies would follow them. Everything was so different. If you went in a farmyard then there'd be the hens running around loose and the bullocks, the cows, the horses in their stalls. You'd hear them stamping their feet close by and snorting through their noses and so on. Well you don't get all those noises now, or the smells. The odours of the stable and the cow yard aren't there in the same way. You only seem to get one smell now, and that's from tractors, which is exactly the same as you get from the motor car on the road, or the motor lorry.

Harvest was a different thing altogether. We used to take harvest dinners out to the field. The men used to work in the fields because the corn was all carted on horses and wagons to the stack. This had to be built by hand, although a few places had a harvest elevator. Usually the men went to the harvest field and stayed there all day. We boys used to help take their meals because they would be working until dark. In a group of men harvesting, if the farm was big enough, there'd be two loaders and two pitchers, three on the stack and one unloading; quite a gang of them. When the wives and the sons and daughters brought the midday meal somebody would go and get a gallon of beer, if they could afford it. There was a whole different atmosphere altogether. Compare that with what happens now when there is just a combine in the field, with one man on it, somebody comes along with a tractor and trailer to unload the corn automatically from the combine, and away they go. When they used to cut the corn in the old days there'd be crowds of people standing round to run the rabbits; farmers didn't mind you doing that. There used to be schoolboys and all kinds of people, all feeling the excitement of it. Then the wheat and oats would be put up in 'shocks', we used to call them, but 'stooks' I think is the proper name, for a week or a fortnight according to the condition of the weather and the corn itself. Some of the corn would be taken down to the stack yard and some of it would be left in the field. Later in the year the threshing machine would come round and thresh the various stacks to make straw for the bullock yards. Even the chaff was used to feed the stock but there's none of that now.

The whole landscape has changed. The hedges which were so much a part of our lives have vanished, and with them the insect and bird life. Even the birds that once you'd think very common have gone. One of my first jobs was crow scaring. Now machines do this but actually they are used more for pigeons. I remember seeing the fields black with crows. You never see that anymore. The work was hard, everything was done by skilled hands and everyone shared in it and in the fun. Everything was an occasion: the harvest dinners, the games, the outings and of course the visits to the fair.

All we'd seen during the year was a horse and cart or the odd traction engine which came to thresh the corn, so that when we went to the fairground and saw the galloping horse roundabout or the Gondola dragon switchback, the showman's engine with all its gleaming brass and electric light, well we thought that was something rare, not only children but even grown ups. I've seen men and women ten or twenty deep round a set of gallopers or standing looking at the showman's engine with the dynamo humming away, and all the electric light. Fairs were a big attraction to us all, we looked upon them as something magic. There was no wireless, no television. We went to church on Sunday and heard our local church organ which was very small. Think of the organ on the roundabout in a place like Walsingham market place, a terrific sound in the evening, with all the gold and gilt on it. There were all the stalls with naphtha flare lights on them and the smell of paraffin which we used to think was nice. There wasn't any candy floss but there were various other things that gave off sweet odours and smells we used to like. There was the smell of the engines' smoke, the smell of the oil; there was the smell of the engines on the roundabouts which were driven by steam. The atmosphere was marvellous. You went home and thought about it and looked forward to the next year's fair because there was nothing else like it.

The music was terrific as well. You'd hear 'The Old Bull and Bush' and some of the old music hall tunes, and when you went about during the year you'd hear the old farm labourer as he was walking behind his horse and plough, humming or singing the tunes. You see, you'd hear all year and every year the tunes that you heard at the fair because they were popular for a long time. Some of Marie Lloyd's songs were evergreens and there was a whole host of them.

35

Everybody used to be singing these few songs for a period perhaps of three or four years. When I hear them even now it takes my mind back to it.

The fair brought us our first electric light, years and years before we ever saw anything like it in the local towns and villages. We didn't get electricity here in Thursford until after the 1939–45 war. Well I'm going back to 1910. So the fairground in this respect was years ahead of its time as far as the village life was concerned. It was something really magical and very wonderful. I can remember it so well now. We have lots of visitors to Thursford now and they're all full of it too. They say 'Oh that reminds me of Pat Collins' . . . 'I remember Murphies or Proctors'. They come along with these famous showmen's names . . . 'I've seen Old Victory at the St Albans and Barnet Fair', and the older generation are never tired talking about it. If you've got time to talk to them they start straight away about it all, even though they are from the big towns or cities. We have visitors from Leicester and Nottingham, or London, who did see other things besides the fairground that we didn't see in the country, but they still remember the fair more than they do anything else, because it really was something. They had a good time, rode on the roundabouts, had a go at the coconut shy and there were swings and a variety of entertainments especially on the large fairs in the cities.

All the new tunes were introduced on the showman's organ. There was no wireless to introduce them as there is nowadays. You heard them all at the fair. Against that background hundreds of people met their friends. Young fellers met their girl-friends on the horses or on the gondolas at the fairground and undoubtedly there were thousands of marriages which started there. It must have been so because lots of people have said during the last few years when the organs start playing, that they were reminded of the fair where they met their wife or husband. The streets were dark then, whereas the fairground was all lit up. They could see each other and there was every chance to get acquainted in some way or another wasn't there? Well, you know, if the horses were full they'd ride on the same horse, in the same gondola or motor car on the switchback, and they could force a conversation. There were lots of facilities which weren't in the normal way. A feller could whistle a girl when he went up the road, probably he could sort of see her in the dim twilight or in the dark and then when he saw her in the light he'd perhaps change his mind. Well he didn't have to do that on the fairground because the whole place was so lit up you could see a spider crawl up the wall, nearly.

We were fascinated by the travelling showmen. Thurstons were the main travellers in the eastern counties. They used to travel in a wide area, as far north as Nottingham and Hull, south to Hove and Brighton, and west as far as Oxford. I think they still go to Oxford Fair. Old Charlie Thurston said that they travelled in fourteen different counties, which was a hell of a long way in the traction engine era. You can understand the lorry going so far, but it was really something to go 40 miles and odd when you remember they had a damn great steam engine with three big loads behind it weighing 30 or 40 tons, and they could only average about 7 or 8 miles an hour; 50 or 60 miles was a hell of a long way, wasn't it? Much further than it is in a modern lorry, or so it seemed anyhow. Of course, the rides were much bigger then. Some of the big scenics were massive things weighing 60 tons and the work in pulling them down and putting them up must have been colossal, apart from moving them on the road. Also you have to remember that the roads weren't what they are now, they weren't tarred. The trailers which carried the loads were on wooden wheels and iron tyres, and they had iron wheels on their traction engines too, which would spin like hell on granite. In Wales and various other hilly parts of the country, they would have to pull the loads up by winch and then lower them slowly down the other side of the hill in the same way, running the back wheels of the trailer on skids and blocks. Every trailer was provided with them, to hold it going downhill. That was a terrific job compared to nowadays. A modern lorry has rubber pneumatic tyres, with much more adhesion to the road, for braking and pulling. There are roller bearings on the trailers now which make them pull much easier, and instead of them being made of heavy timber they're made of alloy, or light metals. Of course the modern rides are also now much lighter and smaller and therefore much easier to move around, to dismantle and build up and so on.

Another thing is that they had to be very careful in the way they took down, loaded and transported the old rides with all their

37

carved woodwork. They used to have masses of sacking to cover up the gold leaf to save it from being damaged. So the movement of the showmen's equipment was much more of a job than it is today. The building up and pulling down was heavier work. Showmen were very, very careful and if you look at the Gondola ride in the museum, you will see that the damage done to the paintwork and the carved work is nil. The carvings are still perfect even though they are very delicate. The least touch would damage the flowers and pieces that stick out. On the figures a hand could so easily be knocked off. Think of those figures where they're playing a harp, or of a wooden band conductor with his arm raised. That sort of thing has got to be ever so carefully moved. I just don't know how they did it. I remember you could have a new lorry in later years and within a fortnight the damn mudguards would be buckled up and the rear lights and number plate bent back. Yet for years and years they travelled those steam rides, pulled them down and put them up, loaded them on to trailers and hauled them miles and miles and miles over bad roads, hilly, with pot-holes and all the rest of it, and yet things never seemed to get damaged. We know they must have been very industrious because the fairs used to go on longer then, until midnight. When you think that after 12 o'clock at night, if they had another fair that week, they'd pull down and load up and be gone the next morning by 9 o'clock. How and when they slept I'll never know.

I remember that Harry Dack with a set of gallopers would probably do two fairs and a flower show in a week. He wouldn't have had long moves, he'd perhaps do a few small villages only a few miles apart, something like that, you see. I think I've heard the Stocks' say they've done the same thing, probably making three moves in a week. But even so that took some doing. Even with a set of gallopers there's some work to do pulling them down and putting them up. You have to get the centres all set right, you've got to pull the centre up to the gantry and each horse has got to be lifted up individually, then there's all the rounding boards at the top. That makes you wonder, they must have worked like hell. There were times when they couldn't have had much sleep. I've heard engine drivers say that when they pulled up for water they'd screw the hose pipe on with one hand and probably be eating a piece of bread and cheese with the other. They'd never stop. If they did stop at all, it would be

Burrell showman's engine *Challenger* (built 1904, No 2651) en route from Lincoln to Boston in 1907 with Annie Holland's show loads. (*William Keating Collection*)

(*overleaf*) 'Charles Thurston's Great Bioscope Show and Ride at St Giles Fair, Oxford, in about 1910. This is the same equipment that went to Hull and King's Lynn with *King Edward VII* and *Alexandra*.' (*H. W. Taunt, William Keating Collection*)

39

to have a quick pint. They'd run off the engine to the pub, down a pint right quick and run out again. They had to because when they had a long journey in front of them there was no time.

Another thing, they were so conscientious. I've heard some of the showmen say that they treated their steam engines like favourite animals. When they'd done a long journey and were weary and tired, they'd rub the old engine down, look up and say 'Old girl, you've done your job well'. They did talk to them, I've seen men do that. They thought so much of them, like the old team men did of their horses. They would be in the stable at 4 o'clock in the morning and at 8 o'clock at night. They more or less lived with the horses. They'd comb them down and braid their tails before they went out in the morning and trim up the horse brasses as though for a special occasion, just to go out on the road with a load of corn somewhere! Well they just accepted it. The teams spent hours in the stable, apart from working the horses. The showmen's engine drivers were the same. No sooner had they got the ride up, than they were cleaning the engines. I've heard them say that at a fair like Cambridge Midsummer where there were several engines, or even Lynn Mart, after they'd built up and cleaned the engines they'd take the mickey out of each other. When the old driver wasn't looking they'd put their hand in the back of the engine and show the grease on it, which they'd find somewhere. Some of them would say 'Look, do you call that clean?' Of course it would be bantering and fun, they wouldn't get wrong about it, just take the mickey at each other in the nicest way. But I think in lots of cases they'd do their best to make their engine cleaner than the next one, because of the banter they'd get from the other drivers.

The same thing happened on the farm. Those farm labourers would go for a walk on a Sunday morning and they'd look at somebody else's drilling to see how straight it was. If there was a stack, they'd criticise it, or the way the hedge had been cut. They'd say, 'Cor, you look as though you want some poles up against that, if you're not careful next week that'll fall over', or something like that, you see. If the drilling wasn't straight they'd say, 'You must have been drunk the night before, drunk when you drilled that', even though perhaps that would be as straight as a gun barrel. They'd take the mickey at each other right and left, like the old engine drivers at the fair. The showman had to be a worker . . . I've noticed that without being apprenticed some of them can paint as well as an artist. The paintwork on some of their things is absolutely marvellous and it wasn't because they were trained to do it.

They were good mechanics too. They did most of their own work on the machines because they had to and because they were damned hard up. When it was a ha'penny for a kiddie to ride on a roundabout and a penny for a grown up, it took a hell of a lot of rides to get very far. They hadn't the money to throw away and had to do things themselves. I think the habit was just passed on from one generation to another. I remember the youngsters. You'd see little kiddies, eight or nine years old, on the stall, touting like a market trader. They were ever so clever with their banter: 'Have a go, Joe'. You know, they had all the old slang, 'Stand back and let the lady have a throw'. All the showmen had their different styles and would do their darndest to get a penny out of you, really work hard to get the ha'pennies. Also if something broke down, they'd have to repair it themselves so that they have the ability to do all kinds of things that the average man in the street couldn't do, unless he was apprenticed to it and worked in the various factories and workshops. I've seen showmen, travellers years ago, do all kinds of things, sort things out when something went wrong. If they broke down on the road, there were no telephone kiosks. There was no motor car to get in and ride to the nearest garage or the nearest workshop and find somebody. If they got in a muddle they had to get out of it somehow or other.

All the equipment had more work in it then, everything was more solid. The traction engines were big things compared with the average diesel lorry on which you can't really see anything. There's the bonnet and the chassis, whereas on an old engine you can see all the moving parts and all the polished brass and so on. Dodgems are similar to the average motor car, they're only a small motor running around and dodging about. The rides of yesteryear were fantastic with all the carved work and the arc lights. No modern electric light shines like that. Ask any of the showmen. Fairs were like nothing on earth, with the old engines parked to drive them. With the arc lights, the carved work, all the gold and the organs, it was something different.

Once at Walsingham Fair the switchback was in what they call the Common Place and there was a set of gallopers in the Market. They're both small areas, with houses all round and of course you can just imagine how the organs sounded. The electric lights naturally showed up everything, reflected by the buildings. Cor, that was a sight for sore eyes. There was the Guildhall, the old magistrates' court-house, and a pub on the corner and the other houses. There's room there for a big machine, with side stalls. As you went into Walsingham the high walls on each side magnified the sound of the organs.

I've been to the Lord Mayor's Show in London several times. That's a real spectacle that is, and about ¾ mile long. There are about twenty bands with all those floats, there's the Lord Mayor's coach, all the horses and carriages and all the lovely brass lamps. That's really worth seeing. The best place to stand to hear the mounted band of the Life Guards is in Fleet Street, because the road is narrow there compared to some in London, and the buildings on either side are very high. Any band marching up there sounds twice as loud as it would if you heard it in a field somewhere, and it was the same when a fair organ played in any enclosed space. The Norwich Tombland Fair used to be in a hall, and the old organs used to echo and sound well in there, just as they did in the square at Walsingham that first time.

It was like hearing a congregation and an organ playing in a church. The building catches and resonates the sound, and no choir would sound the same if they were out in the graveyard. In Gothic times they had it all worked out, because they made all those tall churches with high roofs and I'm sure they were made that way at least partly for the sound. Listen to the marvellous carol service from King's College, Cambridge, on Christmas Eve.

The fairs had a similar effect on me. I've never forgotten that first visit to Walsingham. I ran ahead of the others and turned the corner to see it all: the blazing lights, brilliant sounds, people I knew having a good time together, rich smells, noises, brass and glitter. When I let my mind go back to it there was nothing else, there were no newspapers then, no wireless, no television, just our horse and cart country life and the fair. I've not forgotten.

44

CHAPTER 2

THE ROAD

My boyhood days on the farm ended and I went to work on the road. It was bleak and hard at times, but that's how I earned any money I ever had, and came to know the engines I collected later. I liked the rumbling of the wheels, the sound of the steam, the rhythm of the work, and the sun on the roads stretching across the landscape as we added more stone to them daily. The jobs needed doing, we enjoyed them when we could, and there was a craft to them. I don't think that I would have seen the fairs as I did, or understood the way they worked if I hadn't spent the time on the roads.

After the First World War and throughout the 1920s I worked for the Walsingham District Council, making roads with ordinary stone or granite. We also used the same steam engine to haul stones out of local pits, which were raised by piecework and were all over the district. The roadmen would raise and break the stone, then grade it. There'd be a heap in the pit of 600 yards in length, and we'd haul it out in the summer ready to be rolled out on the roads in winter. Roads were all 'waterbound' then, which simply meant that water was used to bind the stone together as it was rolled out under pressure to make the surfaces. Obviously it was much easier to roll the stone after wet weather and you didn't have to cart so much water about from October until the following March. We used to work with all kinds of rock in this way until tarmac became available in the 1930s.

We would mend the district council roads with the stone as we went along, putting 2in in one place and 3–4in in another. Most of the by-roads were only 9ft wide anyhow, and levels were judged in

'This is a photograph of one of the last days of boyhood. It was taken in 1919. I am sitting on the left with my friend Alfred Page, and we are on the beach having our picture postcards finished while we waited.'

the eye of the most skilled man, who had no more money for his work than anyone else. The most important thing was to have a camber to get rid of the water, and the man who could carve out a road in this way became famous in the district. There was an old man named Harry Flegg who used to do the Walsingham area, another called Buck Long; Joe Grady, who used to work in the Raynham area, and Dusty Wright at Fakenham. They were all local legends and strongly individualistic characters. It was as if they had magic powers. They could plumb a straight line in all weathers, ignore the twists and bends of a landscape, and measure like a surveyor. They were real old-fashioned and rough road men. Dusty was a very big man with a large and famous stomach. The man who worked with him was Bob Monument who was as thin as a linen prop. We used to say that if he was in the army and turned sideways he would be marked absent.

Dusty, being the man he was, tended to be always thirsty. I remember a woman bringing out some rhubarb wine to us, when Dusty was further up the road. As soon as he saw what was happening he came rolling and thundering up the road shouting, 'What have you got? I'm something dry. What is it?' So we had to give him some. After that we decided to play a trick on him, and to make an experiment for ourselves. Later we made believe that the woman had brought us out some more, and we put some water in a jug so that it would look the same. One or two of us had a drink from the jug so that he would see, and sure enough along came Dusty like an express train, and we gave him some. It hadn't reached his lips before his face was contorted with disgust. He spat it out, swore at us and walked away. 'Blast, I ain't water dry', he said, but he'd been as dry as hell when he thought it was rhubarb wine.

Another day a farmer at Toftree brought us a jug of ale, and we were all enjoying it except for poor old Bob Monument, who said that he thought it was too cold a day for cold beer. Dusty was there in an instant, drinking Bob's share, and saying something about it being a poor gut that wouldn't warm a pint of beer. We weren't surprised, because he had the biggest belly for miles, and would no doubt, as we had often seen, have warmed two or three.

We often played tricks on each other, and mostly they were funny as long as they weren't happening to you. Sometimes a man would catch a toad and put it in your food basket. There was one old boy who kept the pub at Hindringham, who always used to bring a bottle of beer with him to work. One morning some of the men were working down near a stream and caught an eel of about 4in in length. They walked up to where old Lingwood's basket and bottle were and put the eel in the bottle. When dinner time came we were all interested to see what would happen. Well, as soon as he uncorked the bottle and put it to his lips, the damned old eel was in his mouth. Naturally he objected to this, and you never heard such a row in all your life. He got hold of a road fork, and was going to stab 'the bastard what done it'. I don't know what the hell he wasn't going to do. That was all done in fun, but he didn't laugh until much, much later. Somehow we managed to play these tricks, and still stay working together as a team.

There'd be three men on each team, carrying the stone from the side of the road where we had left it in the summer, and one other man to spread it, making sure that there was an even 3in camber on the 9ft surface. We always worked as a team, ate, drank and slept in the same wagon, and took a great pride in the roads we made.

We always had to work very hard. In 1924 the roads were re-described as 'A' or 'B' standard, and the one which ran from the Crawfish to Melton Constable was classified as a 'B' thoroughfare, because it was quite an important route and went straight to North Walsham. It had been a district road, but the county council agreed to take it over on condition that the Walsingham District Council paid to make it up, tarmac and widen it to a county standard. It fell to us to do the work with two engines, one hauling the materials out of Melton and Thursford stations, and a roller to make the roads. All went well until we came to the bottom end near Thursford, when the other driver caught pneumonia. For the five weeks that he was ill I had to drive both machines. I had to go backwards and forwards with the engine and two trailers to the station about a couple of miles away, whilst the men were loading and unloading or spreading the tarmac I had brought. I did this until 4 o'clock each day, then I asked the man who was with me as my mate to steam up the roller, so that I could roll out the hundred tons I had carted throughout the day. This meant working until 10 o'clock at night from six in the morning. It was summertime so I could see what I was doing, but I

'Mr Porter, the clerk at Thursford Station took this picture in 1924. The Aveling convertible engine is the one bought new in the previous year by the Walsingham District Council. I had been second man on their other engine since 1920, helping Charley Roll who was the driver. When the council bought this new engine Charley moved on to that, and I became the driver of their 1913 Aveling, the one I bought later. That's me to the left, with my mate Alfred Johnson standing in front of Thursford Station about to take a load of rock slag out to the Melton Road. We were working a 14-hour day because Charley was ill with pneumonia. This engine was sold in 1930 to May Gurney by the Norfolk County Council. Years later, when May Gurney had stopped using their steam engines, Sidney Utting rang me from their offices and asked if I would like to buy it for its scrap value, which of course I did, and it's in the yard now. I'd forgotten all about this photograph until one day, about ten years ago, Mr Porter brought it to me. He'd been retired for a while but had only just had time to go through all his papers and photos. We had a long talk, and couldn't believe that all those years had passed.'

49

was exhausted at the end of the five weeks, and glad to see my friend back at work.

In 1930 all local government was reformed and many powers were transferred from the old district council to the county authorities. This was to have important repercussions for me. The county council did many things: for example, the workhouses were done away with and the buildings converted into old peoples' homes. There was a new health scheme and amongst all these changes roads were taken over by the Norfolk County Council. That was the end of the Walsingham District Council and all the other districts in Norfolk as far as road maintenance was concerned. The surveyor for the Norfolk Council at that time was a Mr Warren, who didn't believe in council-owned equipment. He said, 'You can hire more cheaply than you can buy.' He would hire a steam roller only as and when it was needed. He never guaranteed a regular job, and when the work was finished he wasn't saddled with the cost of buying, maintaining or paying the driver for a longer period. What they didn't need they simply stopped hiring. In this way the council's costs were nil except when work was actually in progress.

Now there was a clause in the 1930 Act whereby all equipment owned by the district councils had to be taken over by the county, whether or not it was wanted. Of course in this particular case Norfolk County didn't want it because of their policy of hiring. Consequently everything they took over was eventually sold at auction. I knew that an auction would be forthcoming, but made an approach with a private bid beforehand for the Aveling & Porter steam roller I had driven as an employee. Had I known it I could probably have bought my roller cheaper at the auction because some of these things made less money than valuation. Mine was an old engine, new in 1913, and I honestly think I would have got it cheaper because most of the older engines were sold for much less than expected, even though valuation was made at virtually 'writing off' prices. I made an approach to the council before their last meeting, but with no success. They had already made the valuation. The Clerk in particular wasn't helpful; he was full of red tape, with a red face to match, and told me that he didn't want to know anything about it. He said that the county council would have to take over everything: 'There's The Act you see'—I almost heard the capital letters—'they may need them, or want to continue using them.' He was fiddling all the time with the things on his desk, and with these fiddlings and formalities he dismissed me, throwing cold water on the whole thing.

So I went straight from his house near the heath at Fakenham to see the surveyor himself, old Bob Cannon, that very night. I stood in the light of his cottage door and told him that I would like to buy the engine. He had the light behind him so that I couldn't see his face, and had begun to give me the same story as the Clerk. Then another figure appeared. It was his wife, passing from the kitchen, who snipped in and said, 'Well there's no harm in you applying for the engine on his behalf and finding out if it is possible.' I'll always re-member the old girl. They were both in their sixties then and he would have been retiring soon afterwards. When I left that night she said, 'Well, you can go home, don't lose any sleep over it. I'll remind Robert in the morning that he's to put your application in front of the council telling them that you'd like to buy your engine.'

I was twenty-six years old and eager to see what would happen. I watched the papers for a long while after that, to see the reports of the council meetings. One day, a few weeks later, there it was, 'The surveyor said that one of the roller drivers would like to buy his engine.' I read the whole thing in a few minutes! 'The Clerk to the Council reminded the meeting of the clauses of the Act and the legal obligations.' Other councillors said that as far as they could under-stand, the county council didn't require any of the plant they were taking over and the information was that they would sell everything by auction anyway. The Clerk was not impressed and repeated the obligations placed upon the council by its official standing and the proper requirements, etc. I heard about it all later. There had obviously been a huge argument among them, but there were three or four who stuck up for me like hell. The Clerk was somewhat sur-prised at the support but countered with, 'Has he the money to pay for the engine?' Bob Cannon, whom I had known for several years, said that he didn't think I would make an application of that sort unless I did have the resources to draw upon. I had more friends than I would have believed, and one of them was Charlie Joice, who had always encouraged me to be enthusiastic and said so at the council meeting.

He was the father of Dick Joice, who is now a presenter of programmes for Independent Television. He had started from nothing, and had been a farm steward long before he had become a farmer, so he knew about struggling for a living. I knew him because two or three years before then my van and engine had stood in his yard while we were rolling the road at Ryburgh. He was having problems at that time with an old sparrow hawk which used to come after his chickens. Well, he went out one evening when I had gone to play cricket with Dick and Jack, Dick's older brother, out in the meadow opposite. Charlie had left his gun there and had asked me if I could use it. 'I don't know about use a gun, I've had a shot or two in my time!' Actually I wasn't sure that I could hit a barn door, let alone a hawk. He told me that this damned hawk was after his chickens with a vengeance, and that he'd been sitting there waiting for him for hours every day for weeks. Once an old hawk starts on young chickens it keeps after them because they are easy prey. That suited me all right. I stopped there with this gun hoping for the best. I was just beginning to think that it was no use and feeling the cramp when the bird appeared. I was fortunate because once an old hawk spots its prey you know it doesn't see anything else. I sat there, half hidden, and this hawk came down and grabbed the chicken. As he was flying away I pointed the gun in that direction as nearly as I could, closed my eyes and shot. To my surprise I had got him! When Charlie came back that evening I had got the hawk. He was as pleased as Punch, and probably remembered all that at the council meeting. Of course the surveyor had had to write out a fortnightly report for the time that I had worked for the council, and these records were crucial too. I was no better than anybody else, but he had never had to criticise me in any of his reports. So, Charlie Joice, Mr Pointer and the Chairman were able to support me with a good conscience, with the result that the Walsingham District Council at that particular meeting decided that I should have my engine if I could find the money to pay for it. If I remember rightly the price was £225.

I had been living in the van for years and being an engine driver I was paid fifty shillings a week, which was a lot of money then. I had saved my money. I didn't smoke or drink. I'd had to be ever so careful, and once I'd started saving I had got into the habit. Anyway, to be honest I was worried about the money for the engine, but

I just took a chance on it. I thought to myself, 'Well I don't know, I'll just have to try and get the money somehow. Perhaps I can borrow it!' I thought all sorts of things. I had such a desire for this engine. I thought the world of it and I couldn't imagine anyone else having it. It took every penny I had to buy it and I wrote straight away to the county council and managed to get some work for it immediately. The local surveyor came to see me and said that I could take it on to the Norwich Road and report to an old fellow named Mr Sexton the next day, which I did.

There was one problem. I had no coal and no money to buy coal, so I had to go and see Billy Howard the fuel merchant at Thursford Station, and hope that he would see things my way. We had been to school together. He knew that I'd got the engine because of the article in the paper, and so all in all, he knew a lot about me and what I would be after. I remember saying to him, 'I've got a job for the engine, Billy, and shall want some coal, but I've no money you see, I've spent everything.' As a matter of fact there were a few things which they had valued separately like the jack, and the sheer legs and pulley blocks, which had come to eleven pounds or so, which I couldn't afford. The council had agreed that I could pay that at a later date, so long as I could find the basic £225. Anyway I told Billy this and explained that I had to work for nine weeks before I would receive any payment. I took the council's letter to him and showed him the terms of the agreement. He was a real mate, and said straight away, 'Don't you worry about that, you can have the coal, pay me when you can.' I owe a lot to the village I grew up in.

At least I was mobile and in business of sorts, though we were only being paid twenty-six shillings per day. We had to supply the roller and driver, with everything found for that figure to match the best tender that the council had received. They would invite tenders from all over the country, and often I would have to compete with a big firm like Price of Lancashire who had over two hundred rollers. They set the standard and anyone local simply had to match it. I managed somehow for a while, perhaps by not eating so much, and worrying a lot.

The first year I worked for the council I was lucky to be with one of their top foremen, the man named Sexton. He used to be in charge of the tarmac gang in my division and of course in those days the foreman himself would pick out half a dozen men who had a good eye and who could lay a road. He was good at the job himself, had been making roads as a foreman for years and knew and respected road-making skills. I say that I was lucky to have a job with him because the best and most accomplished foremen were the ones that kept their gangs longest in work.

One of my first jobs for him was shaping a road at Fakenham in April 1930, before the rest of the men laid the tarmac. I should explain that shaping the road meant above all else getting the foundations right. You see when they tarmacked the road they would put on a layer of 2–3in, which was then consolidated by the roller. The idea was to shape the road accurately first so that they could put on the tarmac in an even and smooth thickness. If they had to put 5in in one place and 1in in another, the tarmac, being very pliable would roll out later and follow the uneven contours beneath. The underlying structure had to be smooth with an even slope, because no amount of tarmac would disguise a pitted or ridged surface. This was the importance of shaping. It was the same kind of skill which had remained virtually unchanged since Roman times. If we widened the road we dug out the sides by hand and shovelled in rock slag or hardcore. Then we would shape it with reject slag, which was a small 3in grade, and if this was done well, the road was ready, if not, all the work in the world was useless. Even then you still needed skilled men to lay the tarmac. Some would still manage to lay a lumpy surface, with 4in here and 2in there, giving you a road which was as good as useless. The tarmac was brought in steam wagons and tipped in heaps on the road for the men to lay and spread. That's all done by machinery now.

My job was also to roll out the surface after these six men had spread it and the foreman had been there to see if they'd done well. He certainly had an eye good enough to see whether it was uneven or not. Sometimes after I'd rolled it they would have to go back and patch it, though a good gang and a good foreman hardly ever had to do that. It was a hell of a job for six men to keep going, and there was never any time to be lost. We would have to put down, level and roll 100 tons every day, because this was the rate at which it was ordered into the local station and we had to cope with it. Sometimes there would be very bad weather, and we'd have to catch up with the

'The engine is a 1929 5hp Marshall which I bought from Cromer Council. Here are Tom Seales, Clifford Chapman, myself and Jimmy Meale on a job in the late 1950s.'

day's work in overtime. On occasions there would be two or three loads of tarmac arrive at half past three, so that it was impossible to get it all down by the end of the working day. We always stayed on to do it though, because otherwise we would have to leave it out all night with warning lamps for traffic. Rather than do this, we'd stay and spread it. It was at least pliable then, whereas perhaps the following morning it would have set hard and been very difficult to work.

We always started at half past six in the morning and went on as long as was necessary, with half an hour for breakfast and half an hour for lunch. By working on the roads we could earn about between six and ten shillings more per week than land workers were paid and the foreman had one more shilling per day than we had. This was the kind of work I was doing throughout the 'twenties and 'thirties, and the roads we made have hardly been touched since, except to roll in new chippings.

Steam rolling was an art. You had to be able to roll out the road with your back wheels and forget about the front roller. Tarmacadam moves and shifts about, especially in hot weather, after you have put it down, and you had to gauge what movement there would be on days of different weathers and temperatures. It wasn't 'still' and you could ruin work if you rolled it wrongly. I would go up the side of the road with a whole wheel or half wheel according to the weather conditions. If it was hot I would have to work very carefully, and it was as though I could feel the surface of the road through the weight of the engine, as if the weight wasn't there any more. Sometimes I would just flatten it in the evening and then get out after it early the next morning when it was cool. There was a lot entered into it in the way of judgement, instinct and experience. The foreman knew whether or not you could roll it, and if you couldn't he'd soon get rid of you and have somebody else. He had to know what he was doing because he was carrying the responsibility for it all. Later when diesel-powered rollers were invented they had an equal weight on the front and rear wheels, and rolling the road was much easier, because the pressures were evenly distributed. The steam roller, on the other hand, was designed and made with two-thirds of the weight on the back wheels, so that they pressed down much more than the front wheel, which was used simply to remove any marks you made as you went down the road.

I got on well with the foreman, and he came to see that I could do my job. Anyhow that's all I did for two or three years. I could and did have a job there at any time. This was of great benefit to me because about 1932 there were spending cuts on the roads and instead of a hundred or so steam rollers working in Norfolk there were only two, three or four, and I was one of those who were still kept in work. Time passed and I soon had two rollers working for the council.

Then a firm in London was in touch with me asking if I had a steam tractor capable of hauling a tar boiler, which was a separate unit. I didn't have a tractor at the time, but I thought that if I took the heavy rollers off one of the engines I could replace them with

(*pages 58–9*) 'The Marenghi 98-key showman's organ. Built in 1905, it was awarded the Grand Prix at the Brussels World Fair and played in a Paris dance hall before it was exported to Great Britain in the 1920s.'

'Some of the engines out in the yard. Fourth from the right is the first engine I ever bought, the 1913 Aveling & Porter convertible steam roller, sold by the Walsingham District Council to me for £225 in 1930.'

wheels and convert the engine in this way into a tractor. I had to get
yet another steam roller to replace the one I was altering, and I also
had to have the iron wheels I was going to use covered with solid
rubber tyres. There were firms then who specialised in that work
and I knew of a man named Bloomfield at Debenham who had done
many showmen's engines, including all the Thurston ones. I rang
him and we went down with the front and back wheels of the
Aveling to have the tyres made. As soon as they were done I was
able to supply the steam tractor for work with a tar boiler.

We started sand tarring at first because it didn't need much
rolling, but as soon as I became involved I discovered that we needed
another roller and I had to hire one, because I simply didn't have the
money to buy one outright. We were paid twenty-six shillings then
for a roller. I managed to find someone who let me have one with a
driver for twenty-one shillings, so I had five shillings a day profit for
myself. I worked at this for one complete summer and also carted
sugar beet for the railway. There wasn't much money in this and we
had to lift the beet on and off the trailers by hand at both ends of the
journey which slowed us down no end. I used the tractor which I had
kept on the rubber wheels and worked with my four trailers, leaving
two in the station yard full of beet, and then going out with the
empty ones. I carried on in this way for the first year and then bought
a steam waggon, which cost virtually nothing, about ten pounds because it was old fashioned even then. In fact it's the old Clayton I
still have. I employed a driver for the tractor, I drove the waggon
and it was all very successful. I loved driving the Clayton and the
basic jobs we were doing.

We did a lot of haulage out of Thursford Station because it was
in the centre of the district. I think the work came to me because the
old man who had worked for them previously, with an old model T
Ford, had let them down, and there had been complaints from the
farmers. The economics of the business were fairly straightforward.
The railway would give the farmer the 'all-in price' which it
would charge for carrying sugar beet, for example, from the farm to

George Cushing standing in front of *King Edward VII*. The engine is fully restored and
painted in the Burrell colours as new in 1905, and adapted as it was when George saw it
at the King's Lynn Mart of 1920.

the factory, then they would pay us for collecting from the farm and delivering to the station. We collected a lot of barley which went on to Burton-on-Trent. We were paid something like two shillings and sixpence per ton. When we carried beet, it was two shillings and sixpence for a journey up to 3 miles, and two shillings and ninepence for a journey of between 3 and 5 miles. It wasn't a lot of money, although the values were different then, and we could get a decent living by working hard. We usually carried 7,000 tons a year, and in one year we did 9,000 tons.

Most of the farms in the area only had horses and wagons, which were no use for carrying tons of sugar beet from Binham or Sharington into the station at Thursford. Efficient tractors didn't appear until much later, and our steam engine and trailers were the best things by far for the job.

We also made deliveries for the railway into the Walsingham area. They operated a 'Paid Home' scheme in which they agreed to deliver bricks or other materials to the site all the way from the place of manufacture. We would collect the goods from the trains at the station and take them out into the country where they were needed. In the big towns like Norwich and King's Lynn the railway probably had their own transport, but Thursford was too small, so they subcontracted to us. You were sure of your money from the railway and the council, even if it wasn't a lot. I had some good men working for me, and as I had the engine still on the wheels I put in for some more work hauling slag and tarmac out of stations.

But the next job nearly finished me. It was at Terrington, which is a hell of a long way off from home, on the other side of King's Lynn. We had to go out there with living vans of course, which are usually good to live in and work from. You could sleep well, eat breakfast and begin work in some kind of comfort. I always liked the feeling of being in the landscape, hearing the birds wake us, or the sound of the rain on the roof. Natural things seemed much closer to us than when we were living in a house, and when it was sunny we could sit on the step to eat our dinners. It was wonderful when the work was done.

Terrington wasn't quite like that though. I very nearly came unstuck because of it. We had the job in February; it set in very frosty, and of course the tarmac took some shifting. We found we couldn't keep up with the work, and got ourselves into a hell of a muddle.

There was ice everywhere, the trailers were sliding, and the tractor slipping dangerously about all over the place. I began to think that someone might be killed or injured. During the month that we were there I lost all the money which I had earned carting the sugar beet, and eventually I had to take a roller over there to steam the trucks out. By the time the tarmac had arrived on the site from the plant the freezing weather had made it like concrete. There had been two or three frosts by then and it became a devil of a job. We had to use pickaxes and crow-bars to get everything away in one piece. We managed it, but came out of it with nothing. I was broke.

The next job was at Reepham, then Sheringham, and all the early part of the summer we had a job, though there may have been a week or two in between. For several years we went on like this, tarring, carrying and steamrolling. There were always chippings to be carted from the local stations out to the roads. The men would put them out in small heaps all the way along, and then a gang of about twenty would work their way behind the tar barrel as it was moved up the road, spreading as they went. All this was long before there were mechanical spreaders. There was plenty of work for the Clayton and the engines, and we didn't think anything would change.

Road traffic acts seem to have influenced my life directly throughout. They were always unexpected and arbitrary, as though someone was deliberately trying to confuse things. The 1934 Act penalised all traffic by weight, and suddenly most of the steam equipment became uneconomic to use. Change followed rapidly, and by about 1936 pneumatic tyres and mass-produced Bedfords and Fords came along. I eventually had to buy some and the poor old steam engine was stood up. I did buy a Garrett steam waggon for £25, but even that we had to adapt by taking off the body and putting on a tank so that we could describe it as a tractor. The licence for a tractor, whether steam or not, was only about half that for a steam waggon. You were allowed 12 tons on four wheels or two axles, and since the average steam waggon weighed 7 or 8 tons in working order, with a tank and boiler full of water, you could only carry legally a 4-ton pay load. After we took the body off the waggon it probably weighed only about 5 tons with water, so we were well under maximum weight, and of course we could haul a trailer as well.

63

The first lorry I bought was a second-hand Daimler, built in 1918. It had solid tyres, a crank start and no doors, but it ran like a top, doing 12mph and 6 miles to a gallon. I remember that I didn't have the ten pounds it cost me at the time, but the man from whom I bought it, who was local, let me pay at the end of the season. My cheque from the railway usually came every Saturday, but sometimes the post wasn't reliable, and there were times when I didn't have enough money to pay anyone. If I had been at all religious I would have gone on my knees to pray for that cheque some weeks. I think that the road licence for the lorry was £25, and the lorry was much quicker than the engines, which were then costing something like £180 to license, so you can see what the pressures were.

I was reluctant to give up my steam waggons, the Clayton and the Garrett, but I had to in the end. The Garrett lasted for a couple more years as a tractor. It was one of the last ones to be built, in 1928, so that will give you an idea of how good it was. It became obsolete before it was a quarter worn out, and it was in tip-top condition when I bought it, because it hadn't been in use for two or three years then. It was a beautiful machine with work and life in it, used for a year or two instead of for a lifetime because of a Road Traffic Act. The Clayton's working life ended immediately, there was no way to use it, though I kept it, and have it in the museum now.

I carried on using the engines as long as I was able, despite the '34 Act, because there were no weighbridges around here to weigh the vehicles anyhow, but even without the Act the steam engine with its trailers would have become obsolete. The process was only hastened by Parliament. By 1936 the signs were clear that the 2-ton petrol lorry was the coming thing, but it's hard to give up the habits of a lifetime, and my friend Bill Jeans was the last man in Norfolk to roll a road by steam.

We could never have foreseen in my younger days that a motor vehicle would ever replace steam. If anyone had told us that the railway would be closed down in the villages, we would have thought that they were mad. Even when it was being done there were people who said it would never happen and refused to believe that the closures were going on around them.

In the early days the gatehouse on the railway at the Melton Road was operated by a family named Lambert. They lived there rent free and Mrs Lambert opened and closed the gate. The railway had the priority then, and she would only have to come out to open the gates for the few vehicles that came along on the road. I used to go to school with her son, and he told me that she was often there all day without having to go out once. Within a few years there was a full-time gate-keeper there and the gates were open to the road traffic the whole time, and opened occasionally for the trains. Eventually the gatehouse was closed completely, and no trains came through.

I was involved with the Midland & Great Northern Railway almost until they closed in 1958, and carried goods all over the area, to Binham, Langham, Gunthorpe or Hindringham, using lorries for the latter part of the time. The 'Paid Home' scheme operated by the railway continued into the 'fifties, because the first tractors that came along weren't very powerful. They were mostly paraffin fuel Fordsons with iron tyres, and it was only when large tractors with pneumatic tyres were manufactured that the farmers began to take their own loads of 4 tons to the station themselves. Then when the pneumatic-tyred lorries appeared the railway wasn't used at all, and the sugar beet we had carried went straight through from the farm to the factory by road. All the sidings we used are closed now, and some of these lorries around here are making five trips a day to King's Lynn. That's all we used to do on a 3-mile haul into Thursford Station. All the loading and unloading that we did by hand is now done mechanically so that the whole process is quicker. The 30 miles to Lynn is considered a short haul now, but it would have been impossible for us in the 'thirties.

Petrol vehicles brought so many of the changes I have seen. The motor car sucked the binder out of the old waterbound roads that we used to make just after the First World War. The flint on the surface was bound together with the gravel and chalk, like the mortar in between the bricks of a house. This was all right for a horse and cart, or a steam engine, but when the rubber tyres of a car went round a corner there would be dust flying about in all directions. The binder was rubbed away to leave the granite underneath exposed, and this would eventually break up. The only way to keep the road down and protect it against the speed of the traffic was to dress the surface with tarmac. The roads were literally torn up by the motor cars, and they needed surface dressing from time to time to keep them elastic. When we first started tarring, we only made two tracks of it, where the wheel marks were, of about 18in each one. We never thought that there would ever be enough money to cover the whole road, and when only one man in ten had a bicycle who could have foreseen the time when an agricultural worker would drive his own car to work?

Everything became obsolete quickly except for the steam rollers, which we used right through the Second War and for a few years afterwards, but I kept them, even the rollers when they at last too were no use to me. The yard became a jungle of engines, an eyesore to most people, an impediment to good business and a hindrance to my family who had to suffer my mania. I kept them because I thought my life had been so wrapped up with steam vehicles and steam engines that I couldn't bear to see them scrapped, especially the ones I'd used. They were responsible for my living, survival, and everything I had done. When the horses had been superseded by tractors I had kept the last old horse till he died. I used to turn him out on a meadow in summertime and paid a man to look after and feed him in the winter for four or five years. I couldn't bear to see the old horse go to the knackers and be knocked down. I had the same feeling for the horse as I had for the old engines. They'd been good servants and had done me well. I kept them long enough to see traction engine rallies start and people buying engines that were derelict. Even then I think I was the first one to restore a showman's engine when I did. There were one or two letters in *The World's Fair* which I think were mocking me for painting this old engine up and so on. Eventually other people did begin to do the same thing, but not as early as the 1940s, when the tendency was to destroy them. Also I think that we were the last ones to work with steam. We've got an Aveling steam roller standing in the yard now that I am sure was the last one to work on a hire job in Norfolk, and of course we continued using them for our own work until well into the 1970s. I had engines I'd used myself and I bought showman's engines more or less direct from their working life, so that all we really had to do was continue maintaining them. As I was using the rollers less and less as time passed, I would ask the drivers to clean the showman's engines in their spare time. We'd be out rolling for two or three months and then in the yard for a week or two, or even sometimes

'Lord Snowdon, seen here in 1974. Behind him are two unrestored engines. To the left is the convertible Aveling & Porter, built in 1913, which I bought from the Walsingham District Council in 1930. To the right is the Aveling & Porter steam roller, built in 1923, the third engine I ever bought, and the one on which I made the journey from London with the "roadster" in 1932.' (*Eastern Counties Newspapers*)

for a month at a time. I had to employ the men somehow. I couldn't say to them one night, 'I don't want you any more until next week', any more than I could tell myself that I no longer needed the engines.

Steam engines were massive and slow, but I felt that despite the economics, throwing them away was wasteful. It wasn't just that the engines were going, but the craftsmanship and knowledge which made them. The vehicles which have replaced them are temporary things, built for speed and immediate utility. I liked the pace of the engines, and the time from which they came, when there was a feeling that things should be made fit for their tasks, and last well. I think too that there was a sense amongst country folk that the machines were tools to help us work the land, rather than the land being there to fuel the machines.

CHAPTER 3

THE LANDSCAPE

All around this small village where I was born were huge sycamore and oak trees on the sides of the roads. Thursford had plenty of woodland and lots of small fields with plenty of hedges; in fact every field had a hedge around it and there were no mechanical hedge cutters. Usually the hedges were cut with a scythe and allowed to grow to great heights. People weren't concerned about cutting them the way they are now and I think we are living in a different era. One of the reasons why the farmers have bulldozed down the fences and cut the hedgerow trees is because the farms have become totally mechanised, with huge tractors and combines. Fences aren't needed anymore to keep in the stock, and instead of cattle travelling on foot by road as they did in my own younger days, they now go in cattle lorries. When I was twelve or thirteen years old I used to drive bullocks to Fakenham Market. I've been from Thursford for the 5 miles to Fakenham with five or six bullocks, checking and guiding them every step of the way. You couldn't do it nowadays because of the traffic, but also because there are no fences or even gates on the fields to either side of the road, and the cattle would be running all over the place. The drovers used to take bullocks from Norwich far into the country on foot by the roads in this way, and the best ones would be known by all sorts of odd names. There was an old fellow called 'Meaty Wright' at Fakenham. The drovers would go to Norwich on a Saturday and perhaps buy forty or fifty animals which they'd drive home. You'd see them coming on the road all night and they probably wouldn't get home until Sunday afternoon or evening. They'd take it steady, and people would keep their gates shut because they never knew when somebody would be coming along with a drove of cattle. I have heard that they used to drive geese to Nottingham Goose Fair from Hempton near here and for other huge distances.

The horses worked the land and if a farm was 500 acres it would be divided into 20- or 30-acre fields, and of course the smaller the farm, the smaller were the fields. The largest ones around here were perhaps 14 acres in size. The scythe only pruned and shaped the hedges so that the countryside was much more like a patchwork quilt than it is today. When they mechanised the farms they took down the fences because the large machines needed more room to turn around and they could cover the large fields more effectively anyway with the four- and five-farrow ploughs that they have on some of the farms. The limit that a horse could pull was much less than the limits of a tractor. Obviously all you have to do now is to increase the size of the engine. Years ago if you wanted more power you had to put more horses on to the plough, and of course that could defeat the object. There was a limit to how many horses you could have, especially on the small fields. So the countryside is totally altered, and where you could see rows of trees and hedgerows the roads are bare. There was a beautiful row of trees on each side of the road which leads to my home here, and in the summertime it was an avenue, like a cathedral of trees, so that you could hardly see the sun through the top when they were all in leaf. The same thing could be seen from Thursford to Little Snoring, and that road is only 9ft wide with a small grass verge. You can just imagine what the trees looked like. That's all gone now. There isn't a tree or a hedge, and of course you can see for miles where you couldn't years ago.

There's a school of thought that says we're going against nature a bit too far because as we knock the hedges down we do away with the insect life, and with a lot of bird life because there aren't the places for them to build nests or the insect life for them to feed upon. The hedges used to catch the moisture for them and when you went under the trees during a fog or mist it would be soaking wet. I think that years ago people thought that green things were a necessary part of the countryside, but now economics rules everything. In some places around here they have had to put up what they call shelter belts, to break up the wind a bit, but nevertheless there are lots of places in

Norfolk that now 'blow'. Whenever there is a dry spring there are winds and conditions like sandstorms. The soil is light and it piles up and the ground is stripped bare. Some say that future generations will curse because we use artificial methods and don't put back into the soil what we take out. As we use more and more artificial fertilizers and cut down the trees and fences, a lot of the land will eventually 'blow', as it did in the 1930s in America, when they were losing agricultural land so vast that it was capable of growing enough grain to fill wagons to circle the earth. Huge areas were lost, and farm buildings were buried. I believe that President Roosevelt planted belts of trees then to help redress the balance.

There are many kinds of insects in the hedges that you don't find out in the open fields, and of course many birds that more or less live entirely in the fences such as wrens, which aren't open air birds by any means. I suppose that one of the few small birds that lives in the open is the skylark, but most of them, like the wrens, finches and tits, are hedgerow and woodland birds. They need shelter both for nesting and feeding. There are so many of them that a list would run for pages and would have to include all the various kinds of wood-peckers and treecreepers. So if you do away with the woodland hedges and leave this vast area of open land, you do away with the habitat that's necessary for most of the natural bird life in this country.

All these things are part of nature and may have a function that we don't understand. I think that we're violating natural things so much that we will have to pay something in the long run, and nature will take some kind of revenge upon us. The life of the countryside has taught me that even the smallest things matter, and that the most basic jobs need care. I remember that in my farming days we never had to spray sugar beet. There used to be a kind of small beetle which protected the beet, but the first sprays killed them, and so having started we have to continue spraying. We've killed our natural allies, destroyed the balance of the world around us, and re-placed it with a really vicious circle. I never did have to spray like that, but nowadays I think most farmers have to do it almost every year. There are many other small changes. There are hardly any frogs about this district. When was the last time you saw a frog? They may or may not be useful, but the point is that we don't really know what we're doing or even seem to care. Even the common frog is beautiful if you take the trouble to look at it. The colours are marvellous and the animal itself is something that we couldn't imagine for ourselves, and yet we dismiss it without a thought.

Most birds are beneficial to farmers, with the possible exception of the wood pigeon because it eats the crops. Even the rooks protect the land in their own way. The lapwing is a marvellous friend, and all of them have a place in the life of the countryside, even if it's one that we don't know of. I read recently that quantities of oak trees in America are dying like the elms are dying here. It happens because a damned small beetle lays a grub behind the bark and within a few days the tree is as good as dead. When you think that a little grub can kill a huge tree that has been standing there for two hundred years, it makes you think. I've noticed several things locally which are reflections of changes taking place throughout the world.

The Forestry Commission have lost thousands of acres of conifers in Scotland because of a kind of moth whose millions of caterpillars eat all the green needles of the trees. They have had to spray this year from helicopters to try and kill them, but not before they have seen miles of dead trees. I've never known that to happen before. There's even a disease on beech about which nobody seems to know anything. I've no doubt that many of these things are the direct result of our actions or clumsy disregard for the way nature works. Perhaps instead of going to the moon we should be studying these things with the idea of understanding them. We are already on a marvellous planet, and we seem to be making a good job of wrecking it. All sorts of wild life have been killed by pointless spraying, and some sprays have been banned too late. I understand that the floods in the Argentine were caused in part by the stripping away of much of the rain forests. Lots of countries are busy cutting trees down for profit. Once upon a time there were areas that were inaccessible to us because of swamps or mountains, but now we have helicopters and can devastate even these places. Japan has more or less denuded the Philippine Islands and the East Indies of timber, because as the populations and the industrialisation expand together, more and more timber is needed. Think of how many square miles of wood are cut down each year to make shiny adverts for us. It's amazing how the world is being stripped. The trees are of course necessary to us for the oxygen they give off, apart from anything else. Unless we are very careful we will commit slow suicide. If they do away with the rain forests in South America, and lots of other large areas of forests in Africa the whole world will suffer. The world is like a human being. If you lose more than one third of your skin you die. The people who really understand it are very concerned to see a change in our way of thinking and acting.

I didn't know all this consciously back in the 1930s when I was planting trees; I was just working in the old ways which taught that you have to care for the land and replace its stock. The things I did were only a flea bite at the problem but the rules are the same. You can't have something for nothing, and although the trees are being replanted throughout the world, it's doubtful whether they are being put in soon enough. Every tree that is planted now will be required before it becomes mature and huge areas are cut down to make what in the end becomes rubbish blowing around the streets. There never used to be waste like that. In the village here in the old days the women would do all their cooking themselves, but now there are packets of everything wrapped several times over. Even the suet, which used to come from the butchers is now wrapped and packaged. Almost everything we use comes in a box now, so we're cutting down trees to satisfy needs which aren't real anyway. Even the most simple person from the village of years ago would have known the silliness of it, because it would have contradicted everything we were taught then.

Although there are substitutes for timber, it's still needed at a greater rate than before. It has been replaced with steel in building, and the railway coaches are made from pressed steel too. The dashboards in cars are often made of plastic in imitation of wood in a kind of longing for the real thing, but we're still using the timber itself faster than we are producing it and we're not thinking straight at all. I've noticed the local effects of the loss of the trees.

I haven't seen a grey linnet or a penny wagtail in the last few years and they were quite common until very recently. All sorts of other things are happening to them as well of course, especially to the migratory birds. Thousands of them are attracted to the gas that's being burnt in the North Sea, and are flying into the flames. I remember though that the rooks used to come over here in their hundreds at night to roost, but you don't see them now. Birds like grey linnets, green linnets, chaffinches and goldfinches are depleted in this area. I don't know whether it's the same all over the country; I can only speak from my experience of the local district. Sometimes I wonder about it, but then I think of the fences and nesting places that have been bulldozed away, and the insect life that has gone and it makes sense, or perhaps I should say nonsense. Once you'd hear nightingales or cuckoos shouting one against the other, but I've hardly heard one this year and this place was noted for nightingales not many years ago. You could stand out there and hear four or five easily within a stone's throw. The nightjars, the woodpeckers, the treecreepers and the tits have all gone. Once upon a time you could see them in great numbers. The sparrowhawks have dwindled, perhaps because they live on the small birds. They used to catch perhaps five hundred a year for their food, and when someone dissected a sparrowhawk that had been found dead recently, they discovered that it contained more poisons than there were in the small birds upon which it had fed. It had absorbed the accumulated poisons of its prey and so died indirectly from the spraying of the land. Sparrowhawks aren't extinct but they are in trouble. I knew where there used to be a nest every year but I haven't seen one there for about five years now.

I'm not clever enough to know exactly what is happening, but I do know that there are limits and relationships that have to be respected. In a small and subtle way we are creating our own Sahara deserts in our own landscapes. The animals which don't move fast enough as a desert advances simply die. If you listen hard enough in the countryside and know what you should be hearing you will understand that something has gone wrong. I used to get up in the mornings to hear the dawn chorus, and noticed one day last year that there wasn't one quarter the sound that there used to be. I thought, 'Where have all the birds gone to? What's happened to them?' When you live in the country you can't help noticing it if you are at all interested, which I always have been.

It was 1933 or '34 that I bought what remained of a 15-acre wood up the road from here. It had been mostly all cut down and was a flat piece of scrub land. There were a few trees left up in the top corner and an old timberyard on the other side of the main road with a shed and a well. It was a Godsend for us because we had until then nowhere to put the vehicles that we were using for the haulage business. I wanted somewhere to put the old trailers that weren't in immediate use and a workshop in which I could make repairs. I added to it in the late 'thirties with an office and a shed with a lock. I covered the yard with a stone surface to make an access for the engines, but most importantly I used all my spare time to replant the wood with trees.

There were only the stumps left in the ground, and of course the bramble and elder bushes had sprouted. They had all to be cut back before I could replant. There was a lot of self-planting stuff which I left. I didn't do all the work myself, because there were times when the business was slack and I had a man or two to spare. On these odd days we would go together to remake the forest, just as later on we found work in remaking the engines. Not everyone could see the sense of what we were doing. There was an old fellow named Sid Grooms who had a little piece of land on the side of the road, and I remember him coming through the wood one day: 'Lord', he said, 'you're wasting your bloody time, you'll be working your bloody days up for those trees.' In a way he was right, because you couldn't see the hard woods mature in one lifetime even if you planted them when you were nine or ten. The soft woods grow faster though, and I've seen them all flourish to a good height, and anyway I don't think any of it was a waste of time. I like trees and didn't want to see this wasted ground. I remembered it as a wood in the olden days when I went to school, and it only seemed right and natural to re-store it if I could. They cut down a lot of those trees again for the Ministry of Supply during the Second War. I didn't ask them to, as a matter of fact they wanted to cut down the whole thing and it was only because I knew a man who worked with the Ministry that it wasn't all lost again. I said:

'I hope you're not going to take them all out?'
'Well they're all earmarked to come down by requisition. You've made such good access. That's one thing that's against you, and the wood is right on the main road, handy for Thursford Station. . . .'

74

I thought it was a bit much that they were especially endangered because I'd made them easy to reach, but anyhow we came to an understanding that they only thinned out the trees, and so a crop was left and the wood remained. After the war we had to plant again, and I've often thought of those wasted years. It was 1944 when they were cut, and so there was a decade of growth which had been lost when they went for pit props. All well and good, but they had to be replaced, and the Ministry of Supply didn't seem interested in helping. I've always thought that very odd that a ministry with that title should be mostly concerned with taking.

I've always liked the trees and hedges. We never did cut any down and I always left the trees which sprouted naturally in the hedgerows. Some people don't like them but I always have, and I've planted them wherever I could. As soon as I bought this house I planted lots, and every year since then I've put in as many as I was able. I planted 5 acres in one spot, and some more at the bottom of the meadow. After the war I worked on another 9-acre site which had been a wood when I was a boy, and had been cut down in the First World War and never replanted. There were a lot of thorn bushes I remember, and the man who had previously farmed it had turned it into fields for the cattle. There were lots of areas where there were bushes growing, and I think he left them because he liked shooting, and they were cover for the game. I don't know what it would cost me now, but I paid for a firm to come along and take out all the thorns. I suppose that they were there a week doing it. The bushes lay there for the rest of the year and the following year we burnt them all over several days, and of course I planted the whole 9 acres with trees. One of the biggest jobs when you plant young trees is the 'weeding'. The rubbish grows up in the summertime and you've got to work in between the saplings, clearing around them. I used to pay an old man to come in the evening and I would go with him because neither of us could have done it alone. We put in hundreds of thousands of man hours in the first years during which

(*overleaf*) Steam never entirely displaced the working horse from the rural landscape; there remained conditions and tasks for which the latter was better suited. Such scenes as this survived until the internal combustion engine ended the centuries-old relationship between horse and farmer

the young trees were growing and needed our protection. When I think of the work! No one will ever do it any more, at least I don't think so, because no one seems interested. Even today I've been out in the woods transplanting, this afternoon, just digging one up from one place and putting it in another wherever they are weak or there is a naked place to be filled. You know what they say, 'You dig a hole and fill it up again, it's better than doing nothing.'

I have put in thousands of trees. Once upon a time you could buy small seedlings for five shillings a hundred. I used all the spare time I had cleaning the land and replanting and now there's some nice woodland again around here. On what used to be scrubland the trees are 30ft high now. I mixed them, so that we have conifers and hardwoods, and I made 'rides' down the middle and round the outside so that you could see the beauty of the various types of trees. I put beech on each side and copper beech at the end. Of course we put thousands of daffodil bulbs in as well, so that in the spring, when they come up, it's beautiful. The timber value will be there in years to come for somebody. It won't be me, because I shan't live long enough. In the meantime I have the pleasure of walking round and seeing the countryside at its best, with all the wild life and the various flowers and so on.

I remember Thursford in my younger days. The park was full of trees, huge oaks and beeches in several plantations. I always remember, young as I was then, that I hated the way they were being cut down. I remember walking across the park to the hall, where you used to hear the bell at night, and how they would play cricket there. The memories all run together like the taste or smell of the place. The estate was broken up, and I saw all those trees that I knew by their individual shapes go down. The woods were lost and the avenues vanished from the roads. The farmers who had bought the land cleared everything away, but the memories didn't go so easily. In the summer we had walked under the oaks and seen them in full leaf, and they had given shelter in winter. I was ever so sorry when they went. I suppose that when I eventually got some land and had the chance to plant some wood of my own, it was too good to miss. All the land came to me through people I had worked with or for, at prices lower than usual, perhaps because they wanted to live there whilst I tended to it, or wanted to continue to shoot on it until they died. So I felt I owed the land something. I've seen trees that I planted in the 1930s grow to 50ft. Each year they get bigger and I can see the results of the handiwork. When you sow a field with turnips, corn or sugar beet, whatever the case might be, at the end of the season the crop is harvested and you're back to square one again. That isn't so when you plant trees or shrubs. They grow and develop each year something new, or into something bigger, more extraordinary, and you see the land grow richer.

A man named Anderson used to own my present house. He and his wife lived here for thirty years or so, planted rhododendrons and azaleas and made the place into a remarkable garden. There was an article in *The Field* magazine once about their work here, and they used a photograph of it for the cover on the calendar for the year. They say that Edward Anderson created the garden from nothing and that he was a genius with the woodland garden. It's been a devil of a job not to spoil it so I've just cleared bracken and weeds and added to it a bit. I've introduced several more species but tried not to overdo it. In some places I've improved it and in others, where I've made a mistake, I've had to take out plants and remake it the way it was. I've just maintained it really because Anderson was a man who knew what he was doing. There were two things which obsessed him, shrubs and birds. He planted all kinds of things in here specifically to attract various birds, and I've left everything and studied the birds myself. I've read books and put in things to attract new migrants, so that it is now almost a sanctuary. For instance, we don't cut the grass outside on the pond meadow. There is a stream that runs through the middle, and I've let vegetation grow up so that it's full of wild flowers, grasses, rushes and weeds which are an attraction to the birds. It is very secluded. There are certain kinds of life which don't like the human race anyhow, so we get wild life that you don't normally see, because of the solitude and the quiet. We have lots of brown squirrels at the moment, but once the grey ones come from Raynham, that will be the end of them.

I let visitors come if they are seriously interested and they tell me of everything they have seen. They come with field glasses and those kinds of things which I don't have, and of course they can study birds from a distance, whereas by the time I get there the timid birds have flown away. I won't let them come here shooting, even at pigeons.

79

Nobody ever shoots here on this place. I like to walk around and feed the pheasants outside here every morning. They're as tame as chickens really, though I don't say they would be for strangers, but I just go out and whistle and up they all come. I have a dozen or so every morning, and there are mallard duck on the pond. There is another pond down at the bottom of an acre and three-quarters. I made it myself and it's full of duck in the autumn. I go there to feed them, and never shoot them. You'd think that the pond had been there for ever because it's so oddly shaped as if by nature, and the River Stiffkey runs down the side of it. There's all kinds of wild life in there, coots, water hens and masses of woodcock. I've done everything possible to make it into a wildlife sanctuary, kept all the rides clean and made new ones. There's some nice walks and woodland flowers which grow well here because the ground is peat to a depth of about 18in. The rhododendrons and azaleas love it and they grow like weeds. There are two or three kinds of heather in the place and three or four varieties of bamboo, some of which are recovering from the frost of last year, but I think that they are on the mend, and the whole place is alive with insects, birds and plants local to the area.

I've tried to let the world go its way and just to repair and restore the things I could. I like to see the lanes the way they were when you could always hear a horse or an engine and the voices of the men who worked them.

CHAPTER 4

THE ENGINES

When I first saw *Victory* and *King Edward* standing side by side next to Charlie Thurston's Dragons at King's Lynn Mart in February 1920, I was amazed. There were twenty or so showman's engines there as well, all in the small area in front of the Globe Hotel in the Tuesday Market Place. The railway ran special excursions from Melton Constable, Burnham Market and Peterborough, and late trains would leave Lynn well into the night so that everyone would have a chance to look around the fair before they set off home. This was usual all the way through the 'twenties. After the darkness of north Norfolk the showman's engine was something of a miracle, and to imagine that you'd ever own one was like imagining that you could own the squire's hall. We never dreamt of such a thing, but things did change to such an extent that when they came on the market, they were just scrap. That too is something you never thought would happen, because people like Fred Bushell started and finished their business with the same traction engine going strong.

If you look far enough back through history there were years and years without any changes at all. For hundreds and thousands of years the fastest thing on the sea was the sailing ship, and the fastest thing on land was a horse. This was accepted by ne generation after another almost without question. The implements changed a bit but the method of using them didn't, and they were all hauled by horse.

Travel didn't change much for generations either. People went across the sea under sail power or even rowed, and on land they travelled on horseback or in a horse-drawn waggon of some sort. We thought, in our younger days, that that kind of thing would go on for ever, and for the generation older than mine everything was the same when they died as it was when they were born, particularly in the villages. They threshed the corn with a flail for hundreds and thousands of years didn't they? And it was cut by hand with a reaper's hook or a scythe. Of course when the mechanical cutter came along that was a terrific advance, but they still had to handle it most of the time. My generation was the last to grow up with the old ways.

Steam engines helped us to do the work, but men were still needed in much the same way as always. The big changes came with the end of steam around this area, and accelerated beyond belief as far as we were concerned. The first signs showed themselves with the appearance of the scrap merchants bidding for the engines from our own villages. King's from Norwich came along and began cutting them up on the spot. I thought that the same thing would happen to the showman's engines, which I am sure that it would have done. I bought them with the idea of bringing them home and simply keeping them, eventually perhaps doing anything that needed doing in repairs, and if I could, just steam them up on occasions for nostalgia and to see them running again. It never entered my head that they'd ever be displayed to the public as a museum, or that anyone would want to come and see them. Lots of people took the mickey out of me. They'd say, 'Oh, another old engine come to Thursford . . .' and I'd hear snatches of their conversation as they went past, '. . . can't understand what the man sees in them . . . he must be bloody mad . . . .' It usually went something like that, and even some of my own drivers said it. The engines were just looked upon as junk. People were concerned with the modern things that were coming along, just as nobody bothered about the horse when the motor car came on to the scene. In fact the horse was looked upon as a nuisance because it had to be fed and turned out to grass and so on. But when every village had dozens of them as the only mode of transport, people accepted them as they did the engines, as part of the landscape. Well, last year when I went to a steam threshing show on the other side of Norwich, you couldn't get near it. I stopped at the farm to ask a man the way and he said, 'Look, if I was you I'd go across the fields because there's half a mile of cars up the road.' There were

'Threshing at Laurel Farm in the early 1960s. My friend Bill Jeans is driving the Ruston & Proctor that we have in the museum now. The threshing equipment is here too, in the museum yard. I have to struggle to call it a 'museum'. I still think of it as my shed. This threshing scene is one that I witnessed hundreds of times as a child in these same fields.'

people there with microphones taping the sound of it, and others there with cine cameras. God knows where they came from, but it must have been from miles around, just to see steam threshing. Years ago when you went from one village to the next, you'd probably see three or four engines at work over the fields, and you accepted it because it was something to be seen and done almost every day.

There were still engines being scrapped long after I began buying them. I remember going down to the Hardwick yard in London and I saw them hauling engines in there and breaking them. One or two people had just begun to buy them, and for six years after I had bought mine you could buy a showman's engine for two or three hundred pounds. I could have bought a famous engine called *Success* for £350 then, or from the scrap yard for only £100 earlier. Of course the price of scrap went up a bit, but I remember also going to a yard in Cambridge much later on, and seeing thirty or forty engines there. I told the man on the gate that I wanted various parts, he offered me the spanners and said, 'Look around and take what you want. Call at the office and square up on the way out.' I looked around as he had suggested and to my eyes the sight was unbeliev-able. Most of the engines there could have been steamed up and in use there and then. There was a big 8hp 3-speed engine which had belonged to Chivers the jam people, and on it were some brass caps that I needed for the safety valves on *Victory*. I couldn't have afforded the whole engine, and it was due to be broken up, so I took the whole safety valve. The engine was useless after that; I bet they wish they hadn't sold that now! There was a steam tractor at the top of the yard, from which I took several parts, and then went to the office. You could have bought a lorry load of parts for a fiver then. They were only interested in the weight of the steel or brass, though I hadn't taken much of that, just the caps on the valve, and the weight of them would be ounces. So you could buy an engine cheaply then, and that is how it was for years.

The first engines that I had were *Victory*, *Alexandra* and *Unity*. Of course they were all Thurston engines and had never been owned or operated by anyone else. The original Charlie Thurston had the four engines that we have now, including *King Edward VII*, new straight from Burrell's works. *Alexandra*, *Unity* and *Victory* were sold at the Thurston sale at Kett's Hill in 1947 as surplus equipment; I think that there were some lorries as well, but I wasn't really interested in them. Funnily enough I wasn't at the sale and the engines were bought by the scrap merchants. One of them rang me up and mentioned only in the course of conversation that the engines had been sold but that one of them might still be in one piece. When he told me the price he wanted, I thought 'Blimey' and I knew I'd buy the lot if I could. I realised that one day would come when there wouldn't be any left at all. They were being scrapped in their thousands by merchants all over the country and yet it only seemed a fraction of time before that I'd been watching them at King's Lynn and Norwich fairs. I was thinking not just for myself, but for

84

'This is *Victory* in the shed, just after the new building was completed in the late 1950s. At this stage we had done nothing to the engine, but we were glad to see it under cover.'

all the other country folk who had stood there looking at the electric lighting and the driving generators, listening to the organs, walking back to the engines and so on. There were lots of people who had loved them. Well, I thought that they would never be used anymore, and I hated the thought of them being cut up, because I had spent so many hours watching them.

At the time of the sale I was buying second-hand parts for my lorries, and it was only by chance that the dealer had mentioned it to me at all. We discovered that they hadn't actually reached the breaker's yard, but were still at Thurston's winter quarters. I think that an electrical firm in Norwich had bought them mainly for the generators, and I had to negotiate with them for a price. *Victory* had made £28 in the sale, and I only gave a little bit more than that for it. I had to offer enough to cover the profit they thought they would have made from the engine as scrap, and the ten or so extra pounds I had to pay was then a good profit as far as they were concerned.

'An aerial photo of Laurel Farm, Thursford, shortly after *Victory*, *Alexandra* and *Unity* arrived there, in the late '40s or early '50s. The museum is built on the site of the buildings at the back, away from the road. In the top left of the farm-building area, behind the L-shaped cow-sheds as they then were, can be seen one of the showman's engines, probably *Victory* or *Alexandra*. Directly opposite the main gate to the farmyard is Harry Bushell's workshop.'

I went up to Thurston's yard and saw the engines there. *Victory* had been standing since 1939 and was rusty, but *Alexandra* and *Unity* had been in use until 1946 and you could have steamed them up to drive them away if necessary. Although I had said at first that it was *Victory* I wanted, when I saw the others I was sure that I wanted them too. I couldn't bear the thought of them going away, and so made an offer, which was accepted, for the three. I can't honestly remember exactly how much I paid for them, but it wasn't so much, perhaps £40 each. Of course this was a lot more in real terms than it would be now, but even so when we were younger and had seen the engines at work at Lynn Mart, we would never have believed that such beautiful engines would be sold like that. They were more magnificent to us than dreams. If someone had told us in 1920 that they would go for scrap we would have thought them to be crazy. It's amazing how it happened. After the Second War lots of ex-army tank carriers became available. There were the huge American tractors which could do the work of a steam engine much quicker and more efficiently at the fairs, and didn't take two hours to steam up in the morning. Steam engines hadn't been made in any quantity during the 1930s anyway; they were on their way out and the war only advanced the process. The big military tractors were very cheap to buy like most army surplus equipment, and that was the end of the showman's engine. Ordinary traction engines were making about a tenner each at the time. King's, the scrap merchants in Norwich, bought dozens in Norfolk for less than that. There was a lot of work involved in sorting out the wrought iron from the cast iron, and they had to be cut up so the prices were forced down. The showman's engines were worth more because they were bigger, there was a lot of brass and copper on them, and the generators were still of use. It was in that kind of world that I bought my engines to use and re-store. We put them carefully on expensively hired lorries with huge trailers and brought them home. All the others were going in the opposite direction to the breakers, where they were worth a few quid. No wonder people thought that I was mad.

I can't recall whether I saw John Thurston within a few days or later at Norwich Tombland Fair, but I remember seeing him one day and talking with him about the engines I was repairing. He certainly knew by then that I had bought three of his old engines to restore, so I asked him tentatively what had happened to *King Edward VII*, the fourth engine in his original working set, which I was sure must be in existence somewhere, and said that I would want to buy it if I could. John said, 'I sold it during the war to a showman named Charlie Presland. I'll be seeing him in two or three weeks' time and I'll mention it to him. I suppose that he'll be like the rest of us and want to replace it with something more modern.' I wasn't sure whether he meant it or not, but he was true to his word, and about six weeks after that I had a letter from old Charlie Presland telling me where he would be for the next three fairs so that I could contact him and see the engine. I remember that I eventually went down to Tilbury, which was their winter quarters and where they were having the fair in the third week. It was the Saturday when I arrived, and, would you believe it, *King Edward VII* was there driving a set of dodgems, and another engine, *Princess Mary*, was being painted by one of the sons of the family. So they were still using *King Edward VII*. It was not for sale as such, but Charlie told me before I left that if it ever did come on the market I would have first chance to buy it. He may have said it because he could see how much it meant to me, and he may have wanted to make sure that I would look after it if I did buy it. There was nothing to do but thank him and come away.

It was three or four years after that before I heard any more. Old Charlie had died and his son 'young Charlie' wrote to me. The old man was eighty when he died and the man we all called 'young Charlie' was probably sixty himself. Age and time are considered differently on the fairground by the working families and so my offer of four years before was not forgotten. Young Charlie said in the letter that he understood that his father had previously promised me the first refusal of the engine which they weren't using anymore; *King Edward VII* was standing idle on their ground at Tilbury, and if I wanted to go and see it I was welcome. I wrote straight away to arrange a date. When I arrived there they had a Garrett showman's tractor *Medina* also for sale, and I finished up by buying both. My friend Bill Jeans went down with a low-loader to pick them up. He told me that old Charlie's wife together with all the other members of the family came out to see the poor old engine being loaded up to come away. She said that she was glad that the engines had stayed there for as long as her husband had been alive, and that she doubted whether he would ever have let them go. Whilst the engines had been in work they were always covered with canvas at night, and whenever there had been a gale of wind the first thing old Charlie did in the morning was to check to see if they were all right and still covered. If anything went wrong with them he would spend any amount of money to see them put right again, however expensive the work might be. He never 'hummed and hawed' as we say in Norfolk, or queried any cost for the engines. He would simply hand over the money to his sons, but if they wanted anything for a diesel engine, it was a different story: 'What do you want that for? Can't you make do? Are you sure you want it? Can't you repair it?' He would make

'The Garrett *Medina* No 33905, new to Mr Jas Humphreys in 1920, before it was sold to Charlie Presland. Although it is being used for haulage, it has all the appearance of a showman's engine. It was specially designed, we think by a German engineer, to produce a lot of power from a small frame. I only wish sometimes that I had been able to drive an engine like it around Thursford in the early days.'

all sorts of excuses so as not to part with the money that he spent so freely on *King Edward VII* or *Medina*. The engines had been the centre of the Preslands' lives for as long as Charlie had been the head of the family, and I knew why they came out to say goodbye, and what the sale had meant to them as they stood in the road on that day in the early 'fifties when the two engines came away to my house. They still kept *Princess Mary* though and used her for some time longer.

I went down to Kent two or three years after that and stopped to see them, just on a whim. Young Charlie wasn't there but his wife and the other brothers were. They said that he wanted to see me, 'It's a good job you called. He was going to write to you. He won't be long.' So I waited, and waited and waited, and still he didn't turn up. Eventually I set off to go, but just as I was coming out of the yard he came riding up the road. The family had come out to see me from the gate as they had done before. 'Hey,' they shouted, 'stop, here he comes.' Of course I stopped, and it transpired that he wanted to sell me the other engine. Charlie was one of the last to use an engine on the fairs. I was surprised that he wanted to sell it and told him so. 'Well,' he said, 'the driver has left and I have to do it all myself. Several people have been after it, word must have got around, but I'd rather sell it to you.' I asked him how much he wanted for it. '£850. There's a spare dynamo, a belt, and a lot of spare rubber tyres. It's easily worth that.' He was right, but I was doubtful because I hadn't intended buying another engine then.

I had a friend with me at the time called Charlie Barnard, and he began to get interested.

'Is it worth it?' he said.

'If it isn't worth it now it will be. It's a lovely engine and one of the last ones made.'

'Buy it then, if you think it's worth it.'

'That is a lovely engine, but I've got four others now, so what am I going to do with it?'

Then I thought as well, have I enough room for it at home? The yard was full of these things and I couldn't expect everybody to share my enthusiasm to such an extent. 'I'll think it over,' I said to Charlie. 'I can always make up my mind later.' I've made some mistakes in my life, and that was one of them. We set off on the road back home, and had gone about 30 miles when we decided to stop for a cup of tea. Charlie Barnard was a good friend, and knew us all. I had helped him move house, and loaned him my lorry on occasions. I sometimes asked him to come with me as a witness to any deals struck. I didn't know anyone better than him, because he was an ex-police inspector. We began to talk again about this engine. 'I've spent enough money on engines as it is,' I said, 'there's the business to think about. I can't do it.' Charlie began egging me on. 'Let's go back and get it. I'll buy it, but you can take it home and buy it from me later on.'

I've always regretted that I didn't do it. He would have done that for me, but I hated turning back. 'Cor blast,' I said, 'we've been right down to Kent today, mucking about since 6 o'clock this morning.'

It all went through my mind, and it was then about seven in the evening, with 30 miles to go back to Tilbury. It was not far, but it was too much for me then. I didn't go back and I never did buy it. If I had thought at the time I probably would have had that engine now. I tried to persuade Charlie Presland not to sell it, and to hang on to it. I would have liked to know that it was still in use, but that's just one of those things. I could have had it for a song, and prices have gone up crazily recently. *Victory* has the original generators on it and I don't know of any other showman's engine in the country which is so complete, because when the showmen sold their engines, most of them didn't sell the generators, but kept them to put into diesels. Lots of the engines at the rallies have generators stupidly placed, of perhaps 60–80 amps, whereas they used to have 280- or 300-amp generators on them to be of any use at all in their working days. They do look silly. I have original showman's generators for *King Edward VII* and *Unity*, though from other engines, and I managed to find the actual original for *Alexandra* by a stroke of luck. Lots of generators had been sold to a wood merchant in Wymondham many years ago, and it wasn't until long after that that there was a sale of their equipment. A showman friend of mine, Walter Underwood, usually known as 'Rhubarb' told me about it, and he remembered seeing that particular generator on *Alexandra*. Off I went to the sale and bought it.

Most of the showman's engines have been sold and resold in their lifetimes to different travelling families, but as I've said, Thurstons kept their engines for all their working lives, with the exception of *King Edward VII*, and even that was sold only late in its life, in the 'forties. The other three were only ever used by Charlie and John Thurston. If you examine lots of engines that are described as showman's vehicles, you will see that they were originally made as ordinary road engines and have since been remodelled as showman's engines by various owners who have lengthened the canopy or put brass uprights on them and so on. All the Thurston engines are genuine, as they were designed by Burrells for the family, and there can't be a set like them left anywhere in the world. Even when they were in use they were very special engines, and sometimes I find myself shuddering at the thought of how close to the breaker's yard they came.

They are probably in the same condition now as they were when they were brand new, in every detail. This wasn't difficult for us to do, because basically they were in such a good state, so that all we had to do to an engine like *Victory* was paint it. It was working in 1939 and had just stood in the yard. *Unity* and *Alexandra* were in use of course after the war, so there was nothing wrong with them at all. There was little needed in the way of restoration as such, because there hadn't been time for them to rust badly. We had to retube some of them, and some of the canopies were tattered and broken about a bit so we put on new ones. Some of them were relagged or had new tender bolts, but all of these things were relatively minor. A lot of work was involved because we had to strip them down to make sure we knew what we were doing, and check to see what was sound. On one or two the chimneys had rusted away but that wasn't too big a job, and we never had to put in new fireboxes which is surprising when you think for how long they had worked. I had skilled steam roller drivers working on all the jobs and the time to do them, in the odds and ends of days when there was nothing else to do.

My friend Harry Bushell was a good man to know and an invaluable help. He had been a steam engineer all his life; he had his own workshops when he was in business, which he never did dismantle, and he kept them going for us so that if we wanted some metal worked on a lathe he could do it for us. He still has the forge there now, and we could have any work done there that you could imagine. Without him anything to do with the shaping of new parts, blacksmithing, forging or tube work would have been much more difficult and expensive. He had all the skills of someone whose life had been spent with steam engines. He never did anything else. When he left school he went to work on his father's engines, and even when he was in the army in the First World War he was still on engines driving a steam wagon in the Army Service Corps. His father, Fred Bushell, had a threshing business, and most of the engines were used for general purpose work. Apart from the threshing they did timber hauling, steam sawing, bailing or shaft cutting. So Harry was in-

'Harry Bushell standing next to his Ruston portable engine in 1959. This man knows everything about engines that is worth knowing.'

'Fred Bushell was photographed on the 7hp Ruston Proctor engine in the early 1960s, a few years before he died at the age of 83. The engine now stands in the museum, and I can't look at it without thinking of Fred.'

volved from an early age in practically every kind of work that steam engines did. He was pretty adaptable. His father recognised his engineering talents and bought two lathes and various equipment, so that they could do most of their own repairs in the summer months at the end of the threshing season. Through repairing his own engines, he acquired the ability, like the showmen, to do all kinds of work that probably would have to have been done by the so-called experts at some of the manufacturers' factories. After a whole lifetime of that you can imagine how useful he was to us when we wanted to restore things in the museum. He was the best man available, and one of the last people who would know what to do, and he lived opposite us. Without him much of what happened would have been impossible.

The only showman's engines I bought were the four Thurston engines and Charlie Presland's *Medina*. I have a number of agricultural traction engines and the steam wagon which, as I've described, I was able to buy for next to nothing because of the 1934 Road Traffic Act. In the late 'fifties and early 'sixties I found three or four Aveling road engines which I bought because I was so familiar with them. The prices had risen then from the ten pounds of the 'thirties, but you could still go to a sale and buy one for eighty to a hundred pounds. The increase in the prices continued, and accelerated dramatically within the last two or three years. You could buy a roller or a whole fleet in the late 1960s for what seems like little money now. I had my pick from a fleet of Eddison Rollers which would have been delivered for £100, and yet within a few years of that they would have been worth thousands each.

I have always been interested in any kind of engine for as long as I can remember. I suppose I developed the passion from being born in Thursford and seeing Bushell's engines. They are among the first memories I have because I only lived two or three doors away from their yard, and we would always see the sparks coming from the workshop until late in the evening, or see the great mass of the engines go past the house in the dark. Thursford Station was also close by, and I enjoyed seeing the trains. I used to think that it was the best place in the world to be a child. The horizon was the perimeter of our universe, and the trains, the engines, the land and the fairs shaped my imagination. In this primitive world an engine driver was held in awe by children and adults, because he had the skills upon which we all depended. Most of the people in the district knew only about horses, and an engine driver controlled something more powerful than all the horses in the village, and we all thought him something special. We identified the man with the engine, with the dark and powerful machine which was the biggest thing in the landscapes of mind and reality.

Maybe this is what fired my ambition to have an engine of my own, not to become important, but to touch the things of which I had dreamt as a child. Most of my living was earned with engines. I have driven them all my life and it was a long time before I became accustomed to modern lorries, which I only did because it was that or go out of business. Even then I couldn't bring myself to scrap any engines, and when anyone else did abandon his, I tried to find room for it in our yard if I could. There were limits as to how many I could take, but if I saw one that I liked I found room somehow. I bought everything that I could and they were so cheap then that it was all possible. I was the only person I knew who wanted them for anything other than the metals. I never bought any as an investment, and I don't think that it occurred to anyone that they would be worth any money ever again. At that particular time I just bought them because I liked them and they were part of my life. They just stood about here, some of them in the open. I didn't bother to cover them up because sheets cost a lot of money, more than I could afford for the number of engines I would have had to protect. Some of the rollers in particular deteriorated standing about there. I had more engines than I could possibly look after properly. Some of the last things I had were two Aveling steam ploughs which I bought because they were typical of the sets I used to see working the land around here, and I had nothing like them. They used to pull a plough on a winch between them as they stood at either end of a field. They were wonderful things in their day. We used to reckon that a man with a single furrow plough and a pair of horses would plough an acre a day. When the steam ploughs came along with their five or six farrows, they could average about 10 acres a day with five men and a boy for the water cart, so they were doing the work of ten men and twenty horses. Because they were more powerful the cutting was much deeper, and thousands of ploughing sets were built. There were

'Here I am driving an Aveling plough engine in the 1960s for a film that Dick Joice made at that time. You can see the cable stretching from the winch to the plough itself which is just out of camera frame.'

'Here is the Marshall leading the 1923 Aveling that I bought in London, on a road job in the late '50s.'

ploughing contractors just as there were threshing contractors, and some of them had six sets to hire out to the farmers in their area.

Though I haven't had to travel out of the country to buy engines, I've had to make long journeys sometimes, and drive the engine back under its own steam. I drove the second roller I ever bought, an Aveling & Porter, from London to Thursford, and I had no sleeping quarters so I just drove it until I got home. If I remember rightly I left somewhere down the Edgware Road at three o'clock on the Saturday afternoon and I arrived at Hempton Green in Norfolk on the Monday night. It was the spring of 1931. Next year, in the spring of 1932, I drove another Aveling from Camberley in Surrey, and left there on the Good Friday in mid-afternoon to arrive at Swaffham on the Monday night. That was a much slower engine, what we call a single, and I had to stop lots of times to get water and to buy coal on the way. I remember pulling into Newmarket Station on the Monday morning to buy some. They were two of the longest journeys I ever did. I'd never do them now . . . I'd be frightened to do it because you see I only had two old lights like hurricane lamps hung on the front. Mind you, traffic wasn't like it is now, and I suppose from twelve o'clock onwards I hardly saw a vehicle of any kind. The weather was all right and a good job it was, because the first engine I bought had no canopy. On both occasions I picked up a 'roadster' as we called them, to come with me, though only by chance. A roadster was a gentleman of the road, a tramp. On the first journey I saw an old fellow walking up the Edgware Road and I said, 'Do you want a job because I've now got to drive this engine to Norfolk? If you come with me, because I'm supposed to have a mate on the engine, I'll pay your train fare back besides paying you for your time.' So I did . . . I was just fortunate to find him. There used to be lots of tramps about then, some people called them milestone inspectors; that was the nickname they had. They rode in the tender with me and of course they were helpful if I wanted to get water because I had to stop at nearly every watering place. I don't know how you'd do it now because most of them are filled in. Even then it was one of my major problems. I remember trundling into Royston, disturbing the quiet of a Sunday afternoon. The church bells were ringing and I stopped outside a parson's house. I was nearly out of water and asked them in desperation if they knew where the next watering place was. It was unlikely that they would know, and they didn't, so I asked them if I could have some of theirs. They were having tea on the lawn at the time, and at first they looked at the kettle, then at the engine blankly. We soon had a system going though and, with the engine standing out in the road, carried the water to it in buckets. I had a pail of my own and they lent me another. They sat there having their tea apparently without minding, and so the roadster and I set about our work. He was dressed in an old cloth cap, with a coat which reached the ground and was tied with string, and every time he ran past with the water he gave the tea party a brown-toothed, over-familiar smile. They smiled back every time and carried on watching the spectacle. I don't know how many buckets we filled, but there were plenty, because I had no idea how or where I would get any more. I probably filled forty or fifty of them and set off again. As long as they hadn't minded I'd made sure of getting as much as I could.

All the time I was going along I was watching the road in case we came to somewhere where there was a pond or a stream to pick up water, and whenever I came to one I would stop and put in more, even if the engine was half full. For all long-distance drivers of steam engines, water became an obsession because of the fear of being without any. I remember collecting water just as we were coming into Newmarket at about five o'clock in the morning. I noticed that there were some water troughs on the side of the road for the horses. There were lots of horses and carts on the roads of East Anglia then and there was always a notice on the troughs: 'Not to be used by Engine Drivers', or something like that. On this one someone had added in large letters: 'Maximum Fine £2 if you are caught.' I filled up anyway, looking continually over my shoulder for an early policeman. I don't know if I can still be fined for this admission, but it was early morning and there was no one about. I stopped the coal merchant, who came along at about eight or half past that morning, and filled up so that I was all right for a few more miles. In fact the coal bought there lasted me as far as Swaffham on the Monday night.

We used those engines for many years and I still have them. They're both rollers and were very useful to us. We never had any serious trouble with them. Of course we sometimes got stuck like everybody else, and had to be lifted out with jacks and the like, but I never did break an axle, which did often happen to engines. That

'This is the only real accident we ever had. The 1923 Aveling was hit by an American service lorry while working near Sculthorpe.'

was one of the major worries, and whenever it did happen you had to take off the whole tender, which was a very major repair. Engines sometimes suffered by the fact of their own weight, and of course you always had to keep an eye on the pressure gauges, especially on a long journey. I have known tubes to leak, but serious accidents were rare. We only ever had one accident worth the name, and if you were sensitive to the engine it would do whatever you asked of it. Most people nowadays aren't conscious of the engines as working machines, and know them better through the rallies and exhibitions, but they were honest to goodness industrial machines which depended for their effectiveness on the skill of the men who worked with them.

Dick Joice and I have had some good times together since we played cricket all those years ago. He did some of the first TV programmes about engines and put on one of the first rallies which took place at Raynham. That was the first steam rally where everything worked. One day, while Dick was planning the event, something happened which set me thinking about it. An old boy came

99

into the yard looking around the engines. He'd been there about ten minutes, when all at once a hooter on the car outside started to blow. 'Cor,' he said, 'I'll have to go, that's my missus.' I walked out with him, and she got out of the car when she saw him coming, shaking her fist at him. 'My husband's worse than some bloody kid . . . Old engines! I can sit in the car and wait for him for ever. He never thinks about me.' She was holding forth like hell, so I looked at her and thought to myself, 'There's a woman prejudiced against engines. She wouldn't ever go to an engine rally.' I was puzzled about what to do, and told Dick about it. There was a whole committee of us organising the coming rally, but only Dick had enough sense to see the answer to the problem of how to attract an audience. He put on something for everyone. There were flower shows for the women, an old-time fair, a modern fair for the youngsters and games for the children to give their mothers a rest. There were bands, a church service with the Bishop of Thetford, a couple of steam ploughs, engines threshing, and a set of old gallopers on the fairground of Laura Thurston. Dick did all the planning and it was a one hundred per cent success. Everything was at work, from pony traps to horse ploughs, and it was the forerunner of the traction engine rallies of today, such as the one at Stourpaine. Really, it was Dick Joice who invented them. Half the people who wanted to see the rally at Raynham never got there. There was a queue right back to Swaffham, and so Dick taught me that there were lots of people who felt as we did about the old lost life.

CHAPTER 5

THE ORGANS

Rallies also led me indirectly to organs, and the first one I bought was the Marenghi. I had gone with some friends to a traction engine rally in Andover, and on the way back we called at a fair just outside London in Peckham, because the man I was with wanted to see one of the showmen. This was on the Saturday evening and the fair was in full swing. Suddenly I could hardly believe my ears, and I thought to myself, 'Cor blimey'. Of course it was the sound of an organ that I hadn't heard for years, since well before the war. There it was on a Botton's gallopers, an 87-key Gavioli. As soon as I heard it in the distance my mind went straight back to when I was eight years old and had heard the sound of the first one. I was amazed, a lump came into my throat, and after all those years I was back again in my childhood. As we came nearer to the organ we could see it more clearly. The ride was full of people on the horses and the sound carried through the crowds above all the shouts and cries. It really impressed itself on my mind even after we had gone home, and during the next few days I kept thinking to myself, 'I wonder if there are any more organs left anywhere?'

I made a fruitless trip to Nottingham Goose Fair in search of one that I had heard about. Two friends were going there and offered to give me a lift, for which I was grateful. When we arrived in Nottingham they had some business to attend to, and I went with them, so it was a little while before we got to the fairground. Well, we found Tom Norman's organ which I had come to see and hoped to buy. It had a 98-key range and stood on the front of a show, playing the tunes as it had done in the olden days, but when we got there the

The Nottingham Goose Fair in 1911. (*William Keating Collection*)

place was full of people. The show was crowded and Tom was doing
a roaring trade. I thought to myself that he wouldn't want to see me
then because he obviously had his hands full, and that I'd leave it
until later. So we went round the ground for a couple of hours, and
went back to see him at the end of the fair. This turned out to have
been the wrong thing to do: 'You're too late, I sold it earlier.' You
can imagine how I felt. I was sure that I would be able to buy it for
a few hundred pounds. The showmen had been scrapping organs,
leaving them to rust or setting fire to them. I think that even Butlin
had abandoned several at the time, so any amount of money spent
on them was considered a lot. I was too sure and I missed my chance.
Many years later I met the man who had bought it that night in
Nottingham, and I told him how he had pipped me at the post. He
kept the organ until he died, and when, after his death, his sons sold

parts of his collection, I think that the organ itself made thousands
of pounds. I rang them at the time and offered what I thought was a
good bid, but there were several others. I knew that the organ
needed a lot of money spending on it just to restore it properly, so I
decided on my limit. I knew some of the other bidders, and I think
that mine was the lowest offer of all. The man who bought it was
prepared to spend any amount of money on it, he was very deter-
mined and I realised at the time that it was no use contesting with
him. He has since made a marvellous job of the restoration, and
when I look at it I think how nearly I might have had it at the
beginning. It was the first organ I had gone after, and I missed it by
a gnat's toe. If I had gone straight to see Tom Norman when I first
arrived at the Goose Fair I would have had that organ now.

Later I remembered reading in *The World's Fair* about a chap in
London who was an organ builder. His name was Mr Chiappa; he's
famous for the small organs he has built, and for his skill at repairing
the larger ones. I scoured the phone book for his number and rang
him to ask if he knew anything about any that might be for sale.
He told me about an 89-key organ which used to be in Jim Noyce's
gallopers, and said that as far as he knew it wasn't needed any more
because Jim had put another in the ride. The price was about £350,
which seemed a lot of money at the time, though it was very cheap
considering the way things have gone. I thought that I would probably buy it, though I really wanted a bigger one, because my mind
went continually back to the large organs on the scenics like Farrer's
Whales and Charlie Thurston's Peacocks or Dragons. I kept on at him,
asking if he was really sure that he didn't know of the whereabouts of
any other organs that were bigger. I wanted something to match up to
my memory. At first we got nowhere, and he was pessimistic: 'There's
only two or three left anyway, and I don't know of any that are for sale
in England.'

I was very depressed. Each time I called him the answer was the
same. Then one morning, some weeks after my last despondent call,
he wrote to me saying that he'd remembered there was a 98-key
Marenghi in Ireland that he'd serviced, tuned and supplied with
music for several years, but that he hadn't heard anything from
them for a while, so he assumed that it was probably standing idle.
He didn't really know whether they still had it, but gave me the

name and address. I was so nervous about the whole thing, that it might turn out to be another wild goose chase, that I contacted a friend of mine called Dr Green who lived in Bexhill and asked him to make enquiries for me. He had helped me before to find some engines. He was a real enthusiast of traction engines and railway engines and the like, but couldn't think of owning them because he lived in a small house in Bexhill, and they aren't the kind of thing that you can put on the lawn or in the garage. He was a sensitive man, and a conservationist who spent time hunting throughout the country for antiques. He contacted the address in Ireland for me, and telephoned me to say that they still had the organ. It was owned by an amusement park called Barry Island and was in store in a large building in Belfast. Dr Green was as excited as I was and we arranged to go together. This turned out to be the first of many journeys that I made in search of organs.

We met within a day or two at London Airport. I had leapt out of bed at 4.00 that morning, driven to Peterborough, where I nearly missed the 6.30 train, was half an hour late into King's Cross, and made it to the plane only just in time. I didn't know the place at all, and got lost on the tarmac. Eventually though, we were making the bone-shaking journey to Belfast. Miss Barry, who owned the park, met us there and took us to Barry Island. It was the usual thing, with dodgems, waltzers and other fairground equipment on a permanent site. I was too excited to take much notice and was eager to see the organ. We had dinner in Miss Barry's living wagon, which I think was German, with a beautiful dark wood and cut glass. We had a lovely meal there, of four or five courses, and then at last we went out to the building where the organ was. I felt that I wanted to break the doors open, and take the organ back there and then to Norfolk. We talked for some time in front of the dust-covered pieces, and agreed that I would have the first refusal of it. Miss Barry said that the organ belonged to the family, and that she would have to consult her mother who was seventy years of age and lived 40 miles outside Belfast. She and her mother would discuss it, and if it was decided to sell they would send the organ to England. I agreed to pay all the costs of removal. Reluctantly, but with some hope, we came away. We were back at London airport that evening, and I was home that night. We had talked of nothing else but the organ

A 92-key Marenghi organ, seen here at Anderton & Rowland's last big show, at Falmouth in 1912. (*William Keating Collection*)

during the journey, and I was home before I realised it. I had been from Thursford to Belfast and back in a day, and was as excited as a small boy at Christmas. I was pleased with the success of the journey and the promise of the organ. That night I slept well and dreamt of it playing in my shed.

Three or four weeks went by before I had a message that they had decided to sell the organ. It would be loaded in one piece on to a trailer at Belfast and sent to Preston Ferry. As soon as I knew it had arrived at Preston, I contacted a firm who had big lorries at Manea, near Ely. I well remember going over there one morning through the mists and leaving at four o'clock from there. It was still dark as we squeezed the huge lorry through the sleeping towns and villages of the Midlands, and as black as night when we went through Leicester. At Preston we barely stopped at all and loaded the crated organ on to the trailer. I remember thinking, 'What have I done? Will I ever get the damn thing home?' It seemed so big in the dark, and also I realised with a growing horror that I didn't know if it would play at all. We struggled on and managed to get back to Manea by midnight on the same day. I came home that night in the small hours and had a nightmare in which the organ had turned out to be a meaningless mass of wires and plumbing. When I awoke the driver was there with the organ on its trailer. We put it in the shed, and there it stood.

At first no one took any notice. We never played it or even put it together until the following January, when Miss Barry phoned to say that they would be coming over to London to a Showmen's Guild Dinner. We arranged that they would come to Thursford to help us sort it out. I picked them up from Norwich Station on a cold January day and we came back to look at it. The proscenium was packed away in the back. It took us some time to unload it, but eventually it was looking something like an organ again, much as it must have looked in the dance halls of Paris in 1905, if a little bit dusty. But would it play? We started it, and it coughed and wheezed. At first I thought that that was all it would do. 'I've done it this time. It's not going to work at all. It's useless.' Then there was a note or two, a thread of a tune, a few chords and then a full song which came out in gusts, a bit breathily. I could have jumped in the air and flown around the shed.

It needed a good deal of work doing on it to make it play properly, but nevertheless I had heard the first tune. There had been no time to hear it in Ireland and it had stood there for five years silent. As soon as I heard the sound I knew that it had been worth the effort, though there was still a lot to do. We couldn't do much for a month after that, and when I came down to earth I realised that it wasn't playing too well. The poor thing was short of breath for a start; and there was something wrong with the bellows. I phoned Mr Chiappa again, and he said that he would come up the first chance he had to give it the once over. It was several more months before he appeared. He had been to Yarmouth to tune Botton's organ in the spring, and called here on his way back. Although I had spoken to him on many occasions on the phone, that was our first meeting. I must admit that I was again quite nervous as he looked at the organ, especially as he seemed to be doing as much sucking and blowing through his teeth as the organ was itself. 'Well,' he said eventually, 'it does need a new blower, and that means stripping out the whole organ, a hell of a big job.' It sounded like a major operation, but I needn't have worried, because he was a marvellous craftsman, and came over one weekend to do it. He was there with his son and one employee for the two days,

George and Minnie Cushing on the restored 98-key Marenghi which was rescued from Belfast. (*Daily Mirror*)

during which they put on the blower, tuned it, went right through the organ, made all the parts play, and made a lovely job of it. From then on I heard it as it should have been, and I was ever so pleased with it.

We have never had an official opening of the museum. People just heard about it and began to arrive. As soon as the organ was playing news of it spread through the village like wildfire, and that signalled our public performances. I just played the organ one night and some of the people from the village came to hear it. It was about a year since we had bought it, and it was playing quite nicely, perhaps because we had come to understand it better ourselves. It was only a small group of people who came but it was an important occasion for us because it was our first audience. It wasn't too long after then that I had to have one of the electricity board's men come to rewire it. We talked, he laughed a bit, and he must have said something later to the local newspaper man, who also came along to see it. In time there was an article in the *Eastern Daily Press* about the organ. I wouldn't have thought that it was exactly news, but it was unusual and the national press got hold of it. The *Daily Mirror* sent a photographer down here, and there were articles about it in most of the Sunday papers, and the *Telegraph*, with the title, 'The Organ in George's Barn', or something like that, describing how I had bought this colossal fairground organ. I still keep the cuttings now. One of my friends, who owns a garage in the village, happened to be in London at the time. He was having his breakfast that morning and looking at the copy of the *Daily Telegraph* that he'd picked up by chance in the hotel. He said he told everybody in the room about it: 'Ain't that a thing. I only live five miles away from this man, he's one of my best customers, and I've got to come all the way to London to read about him. I didn't even know about the organ.' It made me realise what I had started. People began to turn up at the barn to hear and see it, only a few of them at first but then in increasing numbers. I had thought of it only as a hobby, and it still went on as one for a while, with other people sharing in it as and when they came.

In the meantime I still went about looking for other organs. There was one at Erith in Kent, which belonged to a family of showmen named Wooll. It was a big Gavioli which had stood about for years.

I think that Mr Chiappa had told me about it, and I went down to see it on one Saturday afternoon. It was a massive thing, much bigger than the Marenghi, with 112 keys, had stood there for over twenty years since 1938 or '39, and had stacks of music with it. I had a long talk with Maxie Wooll who had an illness which kept him in a wheel chair, and we looked at the organ together. I was a bit doubtful because I thought I could see a lot of work there, but he said, trying to prompt me I suppose, 'Well if you've a fiver in your pocket, give it to me and the organ is yours.' Of course he wanted a lot more for it than that, and made sure I knew it. 'You won't take the blighter away until you give me the rest.' He was quite right to do that, but I still wasn't sure, so I asked him to give me until Wednesday to think it over. 'Well you can leave it to Wednesday if you like, it's been there since 1938 so a few days won't make any difference.' After I left I rang Mr Chiappa and asked him if he'd go down to look at it and give me some idea as to what needed doing and how much it would cost. He agreed to do this for me, and after he'd been down he wrote to say that every part of the organ would have to come out, and that he'd have to have it in his workshop to do it. It had been left out in an open truck in the constantly changing temperatures, in the damp of winter and the dry heat of summer, so that the overhaul needed would take four or five years of continuous part-time work.

That put me off I must say. I don't think I could have gone home with that story. The organ was eventually bought by George Flynn who transported it up to Durham, and he had to do ten years of work on it after all. I can't think of a more dedicated or imaginative organ restorer. He is an artist. A friend of mine called to see him one night, after he had had the organ for about four years. It was about 10 o'clock but he wasn't at the house. His wife said, 'Well, you know where he is, he's divorced me and married the organ.' He spent all his spare time in the shed, but he's a perfectionist who's made a lovely job of it, and I'm glad that he did get it eventually, because Mr Chiappa was overloaded with work anyway, so that the five years would have become ten I am sure. Anyhow I had the Marenghi, and by this time I couldn't think of anything but organs. The sight and sound of them filled my waking and sleeping hours, and I felt that I would go anywhere to find them. It was strange because I hated travelling but I knew that I would have to search for them. They were like mythical beasts that I'd heard were still existing somewhere.

The visits of the organ fans to the collection increased. They used to come along to hear the Marenghi on Sundays at first, and among them was Derek Londrigan from Manchester. He became a good friend and gave me a list of other people who were engaged in the organ business including Grymonprez in Belgium. I think that Derek wrote to them on my behalf, and asked them if they had any organs that were for sale. They said that they had, but that they were all dance organs, because you see this was the tradition in Europe. I wasn't sure if I would be interested, but we went over there anyway and in the workshop was a big Mortier, which they had overhauled completely. It was a huge machine with 112 keys, and was one of the last ones to be built, in 1938. I liked it as soon as I saw and heard it, and finished up by buying it. Grymonprez and his father shipped it over here for us. They arranged the transport and then came over later to build the organ up and put it together. The organ had arrived and I didn't know quite what to do with it, and then the telephone rang. It was the Belgians. They had never been to England before but had caught a train to Norwich and then hitch-hiked as far as Bintree, where they had got stuck. I went and picked them up, and they stayed with us for a few days. We unloaded the organ out of the pantechnicon and built it up without too much trouble. That was number two.

In the meantime we had continued restoring the engines in our spare time. We all used whatever moments we had to clear out the rubbish and rub down and paint them. So we had two organs and a yard full of engines of all kinds. Some were in good repair, and some had plants growing through them, but people wanted to look at them anyway. I suppose the work going on was interesting as well; to see things changing, organs beginning to sound, wooden figures to move, and engines to steam. The place had begun to have an atmosphere of life.

I think, if I remember rightly, that it was through Derek Londrigan again that I first heard of Hank Möhlmann, an old boy who owned street organs in Amsterdam, and of Carl Frei, a most famous and well-established builder of organs. The grapevine method of communication always seemed to be the one which worked best. Derek used to come to see us quite a lot because he was a real enthusiast, and we would talk about and listen to organs all weekend. We eventually went over to Germany together, to Waldkirch to see Carl Frei and find out whether he could help us find some more to buy. When we got there the Carl Frei organ we now have was lying in pieces in the workshop. He told me that it could be rebuilt, but I wanted to know what it would sound like, and asked him if he could give me some idea. He had a street organ in his works which he had just overhauled and retuned. He started it up and told me that it would sound like that but that it could be as powerful as I wanted. The Dutch organ was only one quarter of the size of the Carl Frei, and he said anyway that he could build it to any size or specification I wanted. We decided on a 112-key size as it is now. He extended the front for me, put in new pipes to get the bright sound that I wanted, and made the whole thing into five sections to transport it easily. He was a master of his craft. He seemed to know exactly how it would speak, and he could make a pile of wood, paper and metal into a living instrument that would blow your socks off. I can still remember the smell of the wood and leather from his workshop, which was very small, tiny when you think of what an important place it was in the history of organ making.

It was two years after that when he wrote to say that the organ was finished. Of course that meant going down to Waldkirch again. When I saw the organ again it seemed huge and there was only just enough room to get round it at the back and front. That will give you some idea of the size of the workshop. There were only two people there working on the organ, Carl and his father. As far as I know he had no other workmen, except a young apprentice of about sixteen years in age. The older Carl Frei was still active then, though I think mostly as an adviser, and he died a few years later. His son was then about fifty, and between them there was as much available experience of organ building as you would have found in the length and breadth of Europe. That was a good thing because the organ has been here now for thirteen or fourteen years and it's never been any trouble, there's never been any need to have anything done to it. It hasn't even had to be retuned.

We conducted all our conversations through a local man who had been an officer in the German army during the war, taken prisoner on one of the battle fronts and taken back to England where he had learnt the language. He lived nearby and popped in whenever we couldn't make ourselves understood, which was quite often as you can imagine. They all made wine at home from their own grapes so we were treated to real hospitality and had a lot of fun listening to the organ. 'No, too loud! Softer! Softer!' This was how the conversation went, all conducted through our translator, and all of us becoming jollier the whole time. The home-grown German wine probably improved the tone of the organ, and in a bit of a haze, we left them to complete the work, and came home ourselves.

It always seemed that the things of value that I found were in the back-streets, in overlooked places, sheds and scrapyards. The real craftsmen were always hidden in the undergrowth of cities, towns and villages. You had to look for them and know how to recognise them. They too were a rare breed whom a changing world had often passed by, blind to their skills and neglectful of their imagination.

Now that I had heard street organs I was as much interested in them as I was in fair organs. We heard about a Hooghuys and went to a street fair in Antwerp to buy it from the Belgian showman Albert Bequart. Again the organ played badly and needed an overhaul, but I gave Albert the deposit and he agreed that during the following winter he would overhaul it and rebuild it. He was a real genius of organs, and on his carousel was a 72-key Hooghuys which had been recorded by Decca. Every organ fan who knew about the way an organ should sound had bought a copy of that record, because it was so marvellous. Albert was the man who rebuilt that one and kept it in absolutely perfect tune. Wherever his roundabout was, the organ would play, and as usual, when I heard it in Antwerp, there were crowds of people around it. I thought to myself, 'I'll be happy if he can make my organ sound like that.'

Albert was a truly remarkable man, and such a nice fellow. He told us in broken English of the time when he had been a prisoner in a concentration camp during the war, had narrowly avoided the firing squad and escaped to England. He was landed back in Belgium by submarine, and joined the resistance movement with whom he spent the rest of the war. He came from a really old travelling family, was so friendly and promised to show us other organs and music when next we went over there. He was a really tiptop man to know, and I was ever so sorry when I heard one day that he'd been killed in an accident. He must have been a big loss to the Belgian showland business, because he was such a creative man. They had two carousels with a steam engine in them, side shows and a permanent site in Brussels with a huge building where they could house everything. The roundabouts were all under cover when they weren't travelling, and the equipment was beautiful, but Albert was lost to us after so short a friendship. I was very shocked. I felt that he had been a man who was full of musical knowledge, so that any instrument that he tuned had something of his character. He seemed to have been able to find harmonies and dissonances as no one else on the fairs could, and discover something of the original designer's ideas for the sound. I was very sad at our loss, and so disappointed that he wouldn't be working on the organ we had bought from him. Albert's father told us that his son had wanted us to have the Hooghuys and he helped us get it home to Thursford, where we've tried to look after it and restore it as Albert might have done himself.

As the organ wasn't in good playing order Hank Möhlmann came over to stay with us for about six weeks, stripped out the organ completely and did a terrific amount of work on it. He also told me about a Wellerhaus, which we went to see about 30 or 40 miles outside Amsterdam, and eventually bought some years later. It was the usual story of an older showman hanging on to the organ for as long as he could, and then selling it to us because no one else wanted to use it. The younger showmen were always more fond of the recorded music.

Hank Möhlmann is a typical Amsterdam man. He was born there, has spent all his life there, and had then three or four street organs which he used to hire out to the people who played them in the streets going round with a box for the money. Hank maintained and repaired the organs, supplied the music and kept them in tune, much in the way that firms in London used to hire out barrel organs years ago. I bought the big 121 Decap organ directly from him. He had found it somewhere in a dance hall in Holland, taken it into his works and restored it. I went over there to hear it, and it was in immaculate condition, filling the workshop with sounds, trills and scales. Impressed though I was I didn't decide to buy it then because I thought that I already had one, and I imagined that dance organs were pretty much the same. It was of course much bigger than the Wellerhaus, and as I was looking around it I noticed the name 'Mortier' inscribed on it. It transpired that it had originally been made by Mortier as a 100-key instrument, and then in 1938 Decap bought some of the Mortier patents, took over some of their business and finished this organ off as a 121-key instrument in their own name. As soon as I learnt that, I listened harder, and began to see how good it was.

We arranged to have Hank Möhlmann bring the organ to Thursford and build it for us. It had been standing on the floor in his workshop, which wasn't good for it, so we had to buy a trailer which had been part of an articulated lorry to raise it off the ground. It's a big organ and fills the whole length and width of the trailer.

The last organ we bought was also from Holland. I used to go over on the boat from Harwich. It was an awkward journey because to get to Amsterdam you had to get on the train at the Hook of Holland, to go to Rotterdam first. Since Norwich Airport has been operational I've flown over there, and made the direct journey in forty-five minutes. This means it's an easy one-day journey; we could leave at nine in the morning and get back by six in the evening, which gave us the whole day to see and hear the organs. I have enjoyed all my visits to Europe, learnt a lot and seen many beautiful fairs. I don't suppose I ought to say this, but the fairs in Belgium, Holland, France and Germany are very ornate; everything is spick and span. The way they are painted and maintained is fantastic, and they do make some of our fairgrounds look dowdy.

Thinking about my journeys reminds me strongly of the first time I ever came to fly in an aeroplane. I remember the shock of it so well. There I was cleaning the engines one Sunday morning at Thursford, in a world of my own, when in walked a French showman named Pierre. I think he had something to do with all the big wheels that were in England, at Yarmouth and other places. He visited the collection, and spent the whole day talking about it, particularly the Marenghi, which he said reminded him so much of Paris. He stayed the night with us, and when he left the next morning he said, 'I shall be going home to Paris at the end of the season, in November,. and

I'll take you and show you everything.' He added that he knew of a big Gavioli which would be on an old train ride in a Paris street fair at that time. I thought nothing of it and was very surprised when, good as his word he phoned on a Friday to ask me to meet him at London Air Terminal the next evening at 6 o'clock, because he'd already booked a flight on a Comet, which was one of the early jet airliners. Blimey, he frightened the life out of me. I've said I don't like travelling, and it was all so sudden, out of the blue. I hadn't taken his offer seriously at all.

Funnily enough I was going to London the following day with my sons John and Teddy anyway, to the Lord Mayor's Show, Olympia and the Festival of Remembrance in the afternoon. We had already arranged this trip, and bought the tickets for the show, otherwise I don't think that I would have gone down to the airport at all. So on the telephone I said that I would meet him there at the air terminal, but that I would make up my mind in the meantime about going to Paris. I thought to myself, 'I'm not going. I can easily get out of that because I can pay him the price of the air ticket. That's only £17, and he'll be happy enough to have seen me.' I had no intention of leaving London Airport on one of those blooming things because they'd had a lot of trouble with them, and one or two had gone down. Anyway, we made our way to London as we'd arranged, saw the Lord Mayor's Show and the Remembrance Service and made our way to Kensington and to the Air Terminal. I was hoping secretly that Pierre would have got fed up of waiting and gone on an earlier plane, but of course there he was. We had a meal there and talked because we had left ourselves plenty of time before the plane was due to take off. I delayed as long as possible, had a large meal, extra coffee and played around with the pudding for a long time. 'Oh,' he said, 'you never go to Paris on boats. That's all old fashioned. Always fly. Flying's all right.' The more he said, the more nervous I became. My lads thought it was a huge joke, and I don't think that I would have gone if they hadn't been there. It was a dirty old night with a drizzling rain, and flying was the last thing I wanted to do, let alone go to Paris which seemed like another world away. The ground was giving away beneath my feet. I was so scared. 'Well,' my boys said, 'GO ON', and gave me a push. There was no escape. When we got out on to the airport there were these damn planes launching themselves into the sky, in the dark, in the drizzle. 'Aw Blast', I thought to myself, but I went with him to the plane, still protesting. John and Teddy kept saying that I ought to go, but I was terrified I don't mind admitting. I went up the steps with my knees knocking, hearing the wind howling round my ears, and feeling like one of the Wright Brothers. I sat in my seat, listened to the engines roaring, and waited to take off. Then a voice came over the speaker system in the plane. 'The Captain and his crew welcome you aboard. We are flying at thirty thousand feet.' I couldn't believe it. I hardly knew we had left the ground. The old plane was roaring and shaking, and then all at once the sound stopped. It seemed to me that we simply went up to thirty thousand feet and then cruised down into the airport in France. No sooner were we up in the air than it seemed we were there, a matter of perhaps fifteen minutes. There was a car there to meet us and take us to a hotel, where I left what little luggage I had brought with me. Pierre showed me my room and then said we'd be back very much later.

Then we set off for the street fair in Paris. There was masses of showman's equipment and some of it belonged to him. The fair as a whole was colossal, glittering and moving, making Paris even more beautiful. We pushed through the crowd, with Pierre nodding and chatting to everybody on the ground, till we came to the organ he had brought me to see. The old man who owned it stood there and we had a sort of confused dialogue because neither of us were good at languages, and I don't know if my Norfolk accent translated well. As Pierre had told me, the organ stood in the centre of an old railway ride, and the engine on the ride was electrically driven when I saw it, but it was obviously still possible to drive the engine round the track under its own steam if you had wanted to. It had a chimney with a flared top, exactly like the old *Rocket*, and was going round and round with this damn great organ standing in the middle, which

'The 112 keyless Carl Frei concert organ as rebuilt by Carl Frei in the 1960s. Notice the difference between the styles of carving in the larger and smaller figures.'

'The Gondola Switchback, built by Frederick Savage in the 1890s for showman George Aspland. In its lifetime it has travelled the length and breadth of England and is the only one of its kind left in existence.'

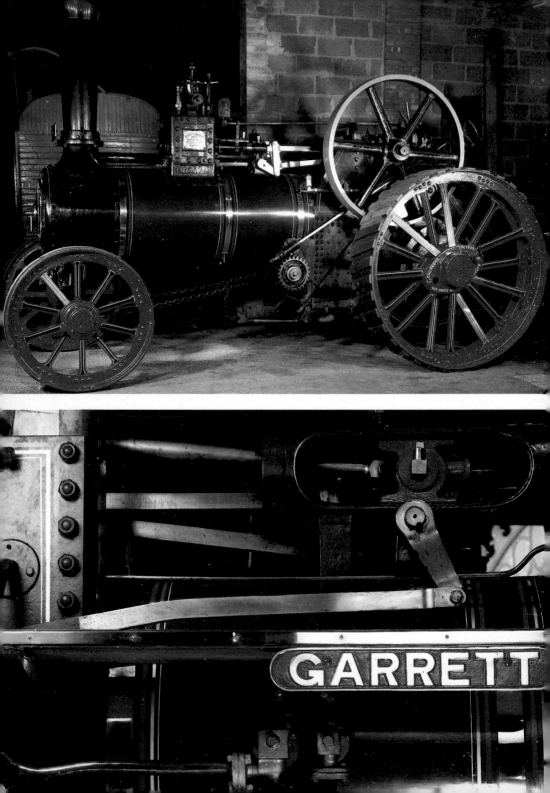

was on a 25ft truck, 8ft wide and that was all organ. It was so big that the key frame was attached on the outside in sort of a little sentry box—there wasn't any room inside for it—but it was in bad condition. A lot of it wouldn't play, a lot of the pipes were blanked off, although it had a marvellous front on it which hadn't been painted for years. There were eleven figures on that front and at least six of the eleven figures were life sized. That front today might be worth £30,000 or £40,000 without the organ. It was a massively carved thing and these figures were really out of this world. I could have bought the whole thing and he would have shipped it over here with his other equipment—he said he would be bringing a lot of stuff over in the spring, to Morecambe, and he would bring it then. I don't know why I decided against it. It was probably a combination of two or three things. One reason was that I probably couldn't really afford it just then, and apart from buying it I knew that the organ would cost a lot of money to do up. It needed a complete overhaul and the front hadn't seen any paint for years and years. Just to paint the front would have cost such a lot of money. I should have bought it though, even if it had been a hell of a struggle because as things turned out I could have taken it round to some of these traction engine rallies and got my money back on it easily. It was empty of passengers when a lot of other rides were full then, and that was one of the reasons why it was for sale. Of all the rides on the fairground it was doing the least trade. It was old fashioned for the time, and yet not old enough then to have become valuable. I wanted to buy it very much but decided, wrongly, against it.

In England at that time, in the mid-'sixties, the steam engines were being taken off the railway and being replaced by diesels, and the loss of the steam wasn't felt until much later. At our place today that *Rocket* would earn a hell of a lot of money and be a great attraction running around on an 18in or 2ft gauge under its own steam. Any-

'*Fearless*, the last engine to be made in the Burrell factory, in 1927. It is a 7hp general purpose traction engine, numbered 4081, and was exhibited at an early Smithfield Show.'

'I love all the machinery of an engine. Such beautiful engineering is rare these days. It's all so very simple, functional and expressive.'

way I lost it. Everything was happening so fast at the time. We stayed for hours at the fair which I enjoyed because I hadn't seen anything like it before. I remembered that the Eiffel Tower had originally been built for the big international fair of the 1890s and decided that I ought to pay that a visit, so we went there and then round the city that night until we finally went in for a meal at past two in the morning. Pierre and old Reimy the showman treated me like a lord, and I was feeling a little the worse for wear. I stayed the night at the hotel and then got up early the following morning, which was Sunday, to see the Armistice Parade. I saw de Gaulle take the salute there. The celebration was different to the ones I knew. There were masses of armed forces marching down the Champs with tanks, soldiers, bands, and then de Gaulle stood near the Arc de Triomphe where the unknown soldier is buried, by the eternal flame. So that weekend I saw both the English and French celebrations of the armistice. In the afternoon we went to Pierre's caravan and were eating there for about a couple of hours—white wine, red wine and four or five courses—because the French really know how to eat. There was too much for me; I was beginning to feel as though I wouldn't be able to move, and there was more entertainment on the way. That evening Pierre had booked not just a seat, but a box at the *Folies Bergère*. We had a marvellous time, what with the wine and the dancing girls, and I saw that the Marenghi that I had at Thursford belonged to the same world as the gaiety of that stage.

When that was all over we went to another of the night spots in Paris and had another meal which Pierre again paid for. There was another cabaret, and it was all going on so that my head began to reel. It was all great fun, but I found that it was exhausting me. The airline ticket that I had was a return for the Tuesday or Wednesday, but instead of waiting until then I decided that I had seen all that I wanted to see, and that I wanted to go home. I suppose I was missing dull old Thursford. I thought 'What am I going to do about here?' I came home again by train. I wasn't keen on coming by air after my first experiences. Pierre took me to the station and we said goodbye the best of friends. I kept the airline ticket as a souvenir of the journey in a Comet to the *Folies Bergère* and the organ I should have bought. It's been restored since and there is a recording of it. I should never have missed it. The life-size figures were beautiful.

John Studt's Grand Gondola Switchback at Cardiff. It was sold to Anderton &
Rowland in 1905. (*William Keating Collection*)

The switchbacks of the era before the First World War all had
figures like that, and if you look in the Marenghi or Gavioli catalogues
you'll find that they had series of figures on them, large and small.
Some of them were cupids, some angels with wings. They were
marvellous to see. The girls were just like Dresden china to look at
with every fold of their gowns more real than silk. The angels' wings
sort of swooped down. They were lovely looking girls with their
arms outspread and wings of gold leaf. In the early days they were on
the bioscope fronts as well as on the organs. Some were Boadicea in
her Chariot, or Britannia, all sorts of things. At each end of the
bioscope front were the entrances to the cinema itself which in some
cases held a thousand people. All the switchbacks had figures on the
rounding boards, if they were only a head and shoulders. After the
First War the scenics had several figures 5–6ft tall on the uprights of
the entrances, sometimes called Ancient Britons, and there were very
few organs that had no figures on them. They were done by craftsmen
who made them to be very realistic. You'd see figures of boys and

girls, and bandmasters who conducted with their hands in time to the music and their heads moving from side to side. Some of the best figures played the drums, like the ones on our Carl Frei. The workmanship and imagination that went into them is amazing. There's so much evidence of lost skills; look at the features of the girls. Some of the cherubs on our Carl Frei were originally on Asplands' show front, and they're so true to life with lovely faces and dimples, they really look nice. With the lights on them and the music around them they seemed marvellous to us, like the most beautiful of men and women. There's not the slightest doubt that they were a big part of the attraction and made us feel more of the excitement of the possibilities of the ride or show.

Figures in modern art are often grotesque. I went to an art exhibition in London last year, and there was a sculpture of a woman there that had a damn great hole through her stomach and no arm on one side, her eyes were lopsided and one leg was thicker than the other. If you see an image of a horse in an art gallery now, it's a cross between an alligator and an elephant. I remember there were two horses on Charlie Thurston's Scenic which had been originally on the showfront, carved so that they were rearing up, with a Roman figure in the middle. They were covered in gold leaf, and they were like real horses, like the one in front of our Marenghi. They weren't painted like a horse, but they were nevertheless realistic, and that is art, to make something which is not an imitation, but feels like the real thing in your imagination. They were as good as the old paintings of horses.

All the bioscope fronts had a platform too, on which they used to have dancing girls and something of a cabaret, which extended the carvings and decorations into real life and you felt you were connected to the painted figures through the real ones. If the carved figures were clothed they were dressed in the fashions of the Edwardian period and are very hard to imitate now. Two of the figures on our Carl Frei organ are modern, and you can see the difference. They were carved by some old craftsmen from the Black Forest who make the cuckoo clocks, and cost me another £100 at the time. They don't really have the character of the older figures, although they do balance the design of the front. They are very austere and there's not the detail in them that there would have been when the art was at its height. Compare them with the smaller figures at the bottom of the organ, which are the results of much better observation and skill, and much more natural in their stance, gesture or expression.

I don't have a favourite organ. They are as individual as people to me just as the engines are, so it's difficult to say that I have a favourite. When people ask me that, it's like them saying 'Which is your favourite colour, flower or tune.' I've been asked many times, but I always feel that I like each one for its own character. However much you may like a tune or colour, they don't exist by themselves. The organs are all so different. I will say that I like the large organs better than I do the smaller ones in general, because a good arranger can get a lot of counter-melody on to a large key frame that would be impossible on a smaller one. The difference between the sizes is the same as between a large and small orchestra. For example, someone can play a tune on a trumpet, trombone, violin or piano, but when you have twenty or thirty instruments playing together it's a different thing. Three or four trumpets mixed with saxophones and trombones give a much richer sound than one instrument. The large organs are of course much more comprehensive in lots of ways. There are not only more instruments, but a wider range of sounds and volumes are possible. There are xylophones and pipes to represent all the instruments, and a good arranger can use them like a full orchestra which contains many smaller chamber orchestras. I often think that it is strange that these organs, which were once so worthless, are now valued at so much money. Prices must have trebled during the past few years on all kinds of instruments, including cinema organs.

Next to the fair organs I always did like the Wurlitzers, because I had listened to the radio and heard musicians such as Reginald Dixon, who was my favourite organist and who seems to have done more broadcasts than all the others put together. I went to Blackpool once or twice to hear him and always bought his records. I don't think that there were any that I didn't buy, so that when popularity of the cinema organs began to fade and the buildings were turned one by one into bingo halls, I began to look for a Wurlitzer of my own. If no one else wanted them, I did. I very nearly left it too late. I remember going to the Empire, Leicester Square, with John to see a film and being surprised by the lovely sound of the organ which played in the interval. Not long after that I heard that the organ from that cinema had been bought by a man who'd put it in his bungalow. I thought that an organ in a bungalow would be a bit much, you know, for there wasn't much room for it to 'speak'. As a consolation I bought a Compton, which was a smaller instrument than the Wurlitzer. I was happy with it until I heard a concert by one or two well-known musicians on a Wurlitzer in Diss. I knew that I had to have one, and the more I heard of it the better I liked it, because I realised that my Compton would never sound like that. I also met someone else who had an eight-rank Wurlitzer which he had installed in an organ chamber over the top of his garage so that the organ played into the biggest room in his bungalow. When I heard it the noise nearly killed me because it was projected directly into a very small room, so that the sound was very loud but dead as a dodo. Imagine one in your front room, and you will have some idea.

Eventually I managed to find the Wurlitzer we now have. I think that the previous owner hadn't been able to get planning permission for installation and so I was lucky to be able to buy it. We had it for a long time after it was delivered in an old building that leaked, and the damp played hell with it. We simply didn't have anywhere else to put it at the time, and when we came to install it we had to repair lots of parts to get it to sound properly. There are two rooms for the pipes and we have just about sorted out the acoustics now. It's a real treat to hear, and some of the best organists have played here. When it was in the Paramount in Leeds, it was thought to be one of the finest organs in England, and most musicians of the 1930s who played it said that it was one of their favourites. In fact Jessie Crawford thought it was the best one he had played in Europe, and most organists who come here now say the same. It's so good that EMI have recorded Reginald Dixon here twice, and he's never been known to record on any other organ except the one in the Tower Ballroom at Blackpool. He has played here on several occasions, and all we talked about are organs. He was at the Tower Ballroom for forty years, and it's said that over ten million people have heard him there. Both he and Philip Kelsall, who is the current resident organist at Blackpool, like to come to Thursford to play and I feel so pleased that they enjoy it here. It must mean that we have set the organ so that it makes a good sound for a large audience as it should do, and the musician can hear and control

'Charles Thurston's Great Bioscope Show at Woodbridge, Suffolk, in 1908. *King Edward VII* or *Alexandra* would have supplied the power for this cinema. The organ is a Marenghi, and the whole front is covered with carved figures. This is one of the best bioscopes ever to have travelled.'

the instrument properly. We also seem to get very lively and receptive audiences here, so that the organists always feel welcome.

The Wurlitzers were made, like the fairground organs, to entertain ordinary people on holiday. They look different, but I think that they complement each other, and that we did the right thing in including them in the same building. After all, the cinemas started on the fairgrounds and the histories of the two kinds of instrument are interlinked. I like to see the audiences still enjoying the organs and riding on the Gondolas the way they always did years ago. That way I know that the things are still doing their job.

CHAPTER 6

THE GONDOLA SWITCHBACK

Our Gondola switchback is the last one remaining in Great Britain of all the switchbacks and scenics, which were the huge steam-powered roundabouts and the main rides on the fairs until the 1930s. From about 1880 all the circular rides, like the galloping horse roundabout and the switchbacks, used a steam engine bolted to the centre which supplied power to the ride mechanically, through a system of gears, with a large cog called a 'Cheese Wheel'. You couldn't see it because it was hidden by carved panels. Then, just before the First War, in about 1910, the showmen began to use electricity produced by the generators on the showman's engines to drive the rides. They had been using it for the lights for quite a while but its use as a general power source had important consequences for the makers of the decoration. All the rides built after the First War, with very few exceptions, were electrically driven and had motors on the axles of the cars in which you rode. This did away with the need for a large steam engine in the centre, and the showmen could fill the empty space with more lights and colour. This is what made the scenics possible. The centre was free for more decoration and more 'scenery', hence the name. The showmen were relieved of the heavy load that the centre engine had been, and the showman's engine became a dual-purpose vehicle, which could tow the loads between fairs and drive the ride when it was built. One man could easily do both jobs, and the rides became cleaner because there was less oil and soot. Lots of people like to see the engine in the ride, but they didn't have to live with it. Through the change new things became possible, and there was room for the large organs to be part of the rides.

Aside from these developments, the scenics were basically a more ornate version of the switchbacks, and every memory I have of these early rides is connected with the first fairs I saw with my mother at Walsingham and Hempton each year after the harvest. Hempton was a sheep fair and there was always a set of gallopers and a switch-back like the one we have here now at Thursford. I visited them every year until I was eleven, and then when the First World War started all the fairs closed. When the war ended in November 1918, the lights of the fair came on again and the first one I went to was Norwich Tombland in the Easter of 1919 to see two sets of gallopers, a cakewalk and the two switchbacks belonging to Barker and Thurston. After so many years of darkness, and compared with the smaller fair at Walsingham, the whole thing was quite an event, with more engines and organs than I had ever seen together. That made a great impression on me, and the following year was even better because I went in the February of 1920 to see the King's Lynn Mart. The 'twenties were a great age for the fair, and of course it was out of this world to me.

You could see the lights of the fairs at Norwich and Lynn even as you stepped from the train at the station, and feel the pull of the crowd as you passed others chattering to each other about what they would see or ride upon. When you came nearer to the fairground there were more and more people until there was a sea of faces, and it was always better than you thought it would be. The gallopers were going round, up and down, lit like the king's jewels, and people were waving to each other and laughing. The night air seemed crisper than it ordinarily was and everyone more handsome than usual. They would shout 'Hello' only to be whisked away in the crowd. Children were munching, fighting and giggling, and everyone was affected by the gaiety of it all. It was festive, innocent and loud.

The Mart of 1920 was full. There were two new machines there, Thurstons' Dragon Scenic and Fred Gray's Motor Scenic, which was one of the last ones to be built by Savage & Co. For many years after Fred had finished travelling the machine stood idle down in the Vale of Health winter quarters in Hampstead. It was a very large machine with motor cars and a huge Gavioli in the centre, which is still in existence and belongs to a collector in the south of England. I remember seeing that organ so well. It stood at one end of the Mart with several life-sized figures on it, and at the other end was Thurstons' Dragon Scenic, with the words 'PATRONISED BY ROYALTY' written upon it in large letters. I think that this was because one of Queen Victoria's daughters used to enjoy a ride there, and from then on, for the rest of the time I saw it, Thurstons always advertised it. Lots of the Royal Family had visited the Mart over the years and it had been associated with kings and queens since the Royal Charter had been granted to it in 1220 by King John. It is a very ancient fair, and I think that you can feel that when you go there. It has begun every year since then on February 14th, announcing the end of winter and the hopes for the coming of spring. Quite often the showmen are under snow there, but they always open, and it's said locally that spring will come within two weeks of the Mart.

In the February of 1920, *Victory* made its first appearance new from the factory, but still unfinished and in a priming coat of paint. It seems that they'd brought it from Burrells at Thetford to help *King Edward VII* drive the new scenic, and I think that a man named Jack drove it to the Mart and also drove it while it was there powering the rides. After the fair was finished *Victory* went back to Thetford to be completed and it came out again in the full Burrell colours at the Easter Tombland Fair in Norwich about five or six weeks later. I remember clearly *Victory* standing there in basic undercoats of paint, and *King Edward VII* which had been to the factory to have another generator fitted. These second generators were called 'exciters', and were used to help start the larger and heavier scenics which were then coming into their heyday. The engines made in this way came to be known as 'scenic engines' and I think that *Victory* was the first to be made with the exciter already in position between the chimney and the main generator, and a crane built on to the tender. Previously they were all converted from ordinary engines like *King Edward VII*. The Orton & Spooner scenics were much larger than the Savage switchbacks ever were. Even the cars were bigger and weighed so much more, so they had to use a crane to lift them on to the trailers when they built them up and took them down. The Mart of 1920 saw the last of the old rides and the development of the new. There were twenty engines there, which was the usual sight just after the war. It was only as time passed through to the late 'twenties that

'Charles Thurston's Scenic at Wellingborough, Northamptonshire, in 1929, one of the last travelling years of the great decade for the steam rides. We used to admire the large carved figures on the uprights at the front, and gaze at them for hours as they stood at one end of King's Lynn Mart during the '20s.'

you actually began to see the new Armstrong diesel lorries gradually replace the engines, and in the early years of the decade we saw the steam fairs at their best.

The Thurston Dragons stood in the main entrance to the Mart, in the premier position, and it occupied the same place until 1930 when it finished travelling completely. Thurstons used to move lots of their equipment by rail between fairs, and in about 1923–4 the Dragons were replaced with Peacocks because there had been a fire on the railway somewhere which had damaged them. So from then on the ride was known as the Peacock Scenic, or sometimes 'Thurstons' Gorgeous Glittering Peacocks'. They were as ornate as the Dragons, and we certainly liked them better than the Whales. Farrers & Halls and Pat Collins came to the Mart during the mid-'twenties with Whale Scenics, and I remember that the Dragons, Peacocks, Whales and Dolphins were the four main rides made by Orton & Spooners in that period. All these machines were the same size, about 6oft in diameter and 3oft high with eight cars, and only the shape of the cars made any difference between them. Nevertheless that didn't stop us having a marked preference for a particular animal on the ride. All of them were ornate, they all had a large organ in the centre and they all had waterfalls, which the switchbacks of course never had. As far as I know none of the scenics survived the changes that came at the end of the 'twenties, and so all we have left are photographs and some rich memories of those glorious days.

All the rides had two or three engines with them generating light everywhere on the cars, decorations and crowds. The waterfalls used to splash down imitation marble steps or rockery of some sort. They were about 2ft wide and carried a lot of water which was pumped around to maintain the flow. Many of the machines were called 'Jungle Scenics', because there were decorations around the outside on all the boards of exotic places, palm leaves, lions and tigers. All the centre was full of scenery which took ages to build up, and the water-falls were made to look as if they were running out of the sides of the rocks, splashing down. They were very elaborate and realistic, so what with the sound and the lights you were taken out of yourself to a magic land. From the front you saw the organ through the big extended arches. You will have gathered by now that I liked the figures on the organs, and Thurstons had some of the best, with four big Ancient Briton figures on theirs. They took your breath away when you saw them shining in the lights. When you went around the back of the ride you saw the scenery all built up, right away up the outside of the truck on which the cars ran, and then further round you could see the waterfall. You can just imagine what that looked like illuminated at night, with the brightness on the water as it splashed down. There was a lot of illusion, so that you lost your sense of the scale of the ride, and your sense of place and time soon followed.

Before the First War most of the switchbacks relied on a lot of carving for decoration, but the panels of the scenics were flatter with more paint work and fretwork like cut outs of leaves. The rounding boards which went along the top edge of the ride had a serrated border instead of heavily carved domes and droppers like the gallopers had, and were painted to represent jungle in a more two-dimensional style, which was less sculptural. It was a different kind of image altogether to the switchbacks, although you still went round up the two hills and down the valleys with eight cars. There were many more pictures and the effect of them together with the water, the movement of the ride and the sound of the organ was to change completely the place where you were.

The scenics had five double seats in each car, whereas the switchbacks had only four, and they were bigger by about 1oft, and that extra width also helped to make them a more exciting ride. I saw the Thurston scenic regularly after that; I never missed a Lynn Mart, Norwich Tombland or Christmas Fair between 1920 and 1930. By the beginning of the 'thirties they had stood up the big rides and the organs, because by then the dodgems had come along with their record players. The engines were in use for a while—you could still find several engines at the big fairs right up until the commencement of the Second War. The steam rides themselves vanished virtually overnight and of course in their place came the novelty rides which were much smaller, easier to travel and much faster, which is what the younger generation wanted, because we were approaching the jet age. There were more motor cars and motor bikes on the road, aeroplanes were developing and becoming more common. Everything was going much faster and the old type of scenic or switchback just wasn't fast enough any more. The rides changed from being a journey which you went on in your imagination, to a machine which gave you the physical experience of flight of one kind or another, and flirted with the dangers of speed. Now it is even worse than ever; the showmen tell me that you've nearly got to take off to give them fun. Even on our old switchback down at the museum all the younger ones always shout 'Faster! Faster! Faster!' You could never go fast enough for them.

How different it used to be. The fairground was rich with ornament, carved work and gold leaf, with the traction engines right to the fore, and fairs were crowded with people of all ages. I remember that at Lynn Mart you had great difficulty in getting round the ground at all on Tuesdays and Saturdays. You had to push your way through. I've sometimes seen huge queues to the rides even when there were several of them to enjoy. Every one was packed with people running to get on. There was nothing like it and there was no competition from television. Everything has changed since then of course. People still go to the fairground, but I think that today it is more for the youngsters, whereas once upon a time elderly people could go and have a good time there too. Fairgrounds are for teenagers now, with pop records and disco rides.

In the 1920s we used to go out to meet the rides when we could as they came into the town. The loaded trailers were a real sight as they came into view. I should think that the big scenics had ten or a dozen loads. You see the organ was one load for a start and then there were all the track and the cars. Even if they had packed four cars into a trailer there would be two big trucks to pull. They were massive things, all very mysterious. We used to wonder what kind of rides there were under the canvas, and whether they were new cars or animals. I have stood with the crowds around the engines. I was only in my teens and twenties then, but there were men of between forty and fifty interested enough to stand there just to watch them chugging away, and see the flow of the power to the rides.

That's all past now but it's the background which made me want to buy the Gondola switchback when it became available in recent years. People had started coming to the museum and we had quite a following for the organs by the late 'seventies. The interest in our collection had grown up with the passion for steam engine rallies which were being organised all over the country, in greater numbers as the years went by. At first the exhibits were the ordinary working engines, but the showman's engines soon made their appearance and became the biggest attraction because there was more to look at. Things had come round full circle, and younger people began to look at the engines as we had done. As rallies became more established, organs began to appear, small ones at first, then larger ones, and in the end people began to stage complete fairs. There were galloping horses again, brought out of retirement, and soon no rally was complete without them. Lots of societies had started related to the new interest, and there was one of them in particular which was important for me. It was a friendship society which had been one of the first to start, and had been founded I think by Father Greville who had been a secretary of the Showmen's Guild. The society had an 'Old Time Fair' at White Waltham near Maidenhead. It was a terrific thing, and Coles' switchback was there on damn great trailers of about 30ft in length. I hadn't seen anything like it since my youth. I think I am right in saying that some of the loads used to travel by rail, or had done in the past, because the trailers had small wheels built so that they could be easily adapted for rail or road use. The trailers which went on the road would have the lighter sections of the ride packed up high on them, and I think that there would have been three traction engine loads altogether, so that the railway would have been a great help. You have to remember that even small towns had a railway station earlier in the century and the big rides didn't usually do the smaller one day flower shows, but kept to the towns where they knew there were crowds enough to make it a good-sized fair.

I was interested to see the switchback at the rally because I had never really seen one being built before. Although I had seen so many at fairs in my early youth, I had only been able to go at week-ends or on the Bank Holidays when I had finished work, and by then the rides were all in action. So here, after many years had past, was a chance to think again about the fairs as I had known them. It was like another piece of a jigsaw that I had been trying to place for a long time. All these things gave substance to my memories and brought back new ones. It was as though the rallies were a new sprouting of a tradition which we all thought was lost. After those early rallies, new audiences began to discover the charm of the old rides. There were still Jim Noyce's gallopers, steam yachts, bioscope shows, engines, stalls and many more things which had not been lost. All the big rallies after that first one had gallopers, chairoplanes or a cakewalk, and if they were lucky they had Percy Cole's switchback which was the only one of its kind left in the country. The only other ride in existence which was similar had belonged to the Mannings at Southsea, and had been exported to America. It was a spinning top switchback which had travelled around the rallies for a year and then become too valuable to work. It went to the other side of the Atlantic like so much other fairground equipment had before, and I don't think that we shall see that again. Percy Cole resisted the temptation to sell his ride because he thought that the place where it belonged was on a fairground, working for a living, and he used to take it all across the West Country to the different fairs, including White Waltham. I may have seen the ride in my school-days at

King's Lynn because it was owned by Asplands then and travelled all over the eastern counties before the Coles bought it in the mid-'thirties.

After the rally at White Waltham, events like it became larger and more numerous. The Cole switchback, with one or sometimes two sets of gallopers, was always down at Stourpaine, which was one of the biggest rallies in the country, and that's the show where I became involved with it. I used to go to Stourpaine because I thought then, and still do think now, that it is one of the best, if not the best rally in the country. Everything works there. They don't play about, they don't have musical chairs and all that nonsense. They do real threshing or ploughing and they always have a big fair there. It's terrific. Apart from the old rides they have modern ones as well. There's nothing wrong with that because it suits the younger generation, and everyone there feels that they can have a good time. History seems to be repeating itself through this mixture of the old and new, so that far from being a shadow of the past, Stourpaine now has one of the biggest fairs of any kind in the country. They even have a circus there just as the fairs originally had, and everything through to the newest things.

I came to know the Cole switchback very well through my annual visits, though it never crossed my mind that I might buy it, because I thought that it would simply continue to travel with the Cole family. After I had seen it there for a few years, there began to be rumours, whether true or not I don't know, that Disneyland was after it, and that someone else wanted the organ. I think there must have been some truth in the stories because after we had eventually bought it, a collector from the south of England came along one day

'This is the Ruston & Proctor 7hp engine driven by Bill Jeans and Fred Bushell in the photographs of threshing in the 1960s. It was built in 1910 and exhibited at the Suffolk Show in the same year. This engine could pull up to 25 tons and was used for many kinds of agricultural work.'

'*Victory* is one of the most magnificent showman's engines ever made. It is an 8hp 3-speed Burrell, manufactured as a full scenic engine to drive the organ and provide electricity for the new Dragon Scenic which was built for the Thurston family. The engine appeared for the first time at Lynn Mart in 1920, where I first saw the engine and ride together.'

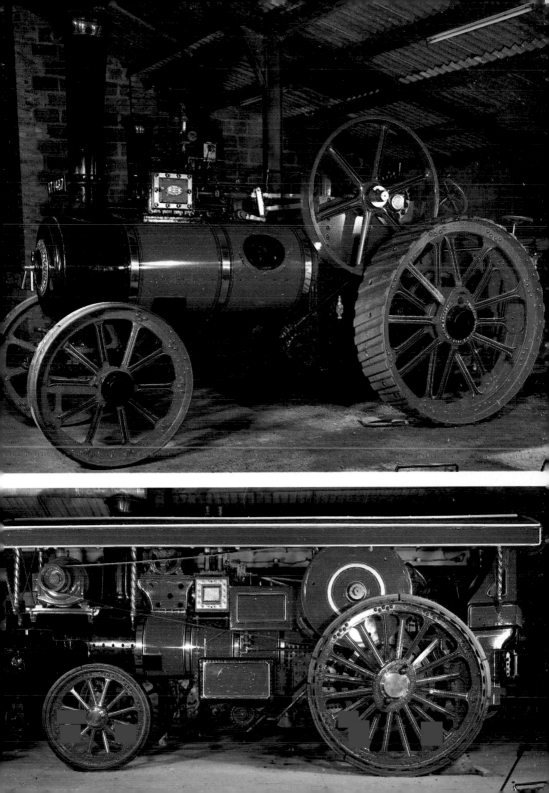

'The Clayton 4hp 3-speed steam waggon was designed as a three-way tipper, so that the rear body could be unloaded by tipping in any of three directions, to either side or backwards, by the insertion or removal of different pins on the hinges.'

and said that he didn't know how we had got it as he had been trying to buy it for ten years.

Michael Oliver, who is secretary of the Dorset club and organises the rally had told me that the ride had been packed away, and that the air was thick with rumours that it might be sold. He took me down to see Percy Cole whom he knew very well, to Ilminster where I saw the family for the first time. I had obviously gone with the idea of buying the ride, and we came to an agreement that very day. Although I hadn't ever met Percy Cole before, we got on very well. I didn't ask a lot of questions. I only went there once and took the chance as it came, because I didn't think it would come twice. Percy had obviously seen me before when he had been to Thursford with the Showmen's Guild bi-annual dinner dance. A visit was usual when the eastern section of the guild held the occasion; they would all come down to see the organs and the engines because there wasn't anything like it anywhere in the rest of the country, and showmen from the Midlands, London or Scotland would come to have an evening here. I should think that Michael Oliver had told Percy that if the ride came to Thursford it would never be broken up or go abroad. It seems more than likely, and although I don't know the Coles, they knew all about me, so that I didn't need to say much. They knew I would look after the ride. It's as simple as that. Most people at the time would have bought it to sell to the highest bidder from abroad, or in pieces to make more money. The sale really set the preservation world alight. It was a surprise to many people who would have liked to buy it, or even have the organ out of it. There was a huge article in the magazine *The World's Fair*, with photos of the trailers being unloaded in Thursford, and altogether it was a big event for us all.

When the machine arrived on all the trailers, we discovered that the museum wasn't big enough to hold it, so we had to build a huge extension on the shed. When the ride is built up, it is very high and 50ft across. Obviously we had to leave room for people to see it properly, and to be able to walk round it. We also wanted to place the showman's engines beside it to bring it to life a bit. It was there a year at least before we could even start to build it up. Johnny Cole came and did it for us, and Anglia Television came along to film it all, so it took much longer than it would otherwise have done. The place was full of photographers and producers, and everything had to be done in a way that would look best for the cameras and the lights. At best it would have taken ages because there were nine loads on big trucks and one of the biggest lorries I have ever seen. The whole business of moving it was expensive because it had to come all the way from the West Country and travel slowly.

What impressed me most of all was the condition of it. It's nearly a hundred years old, has been erected and dismantled thousands of times and yet there is hardly a mark on it. I knew that there was a lot of cloth used to wrap up the ride but I hadn't realised that each piece was individually wrapped. Everything was stacked one on top of the other on the trucks and of course there was a lot of movement on the roads as they went along towing the trucks with the engines. If anything had been put on in the wrong order or out of place the whole lot would have collapsed on the road. They never got it wrong in all those years, and all the gold and painted work has stayed good. The old rides were difficult to move because they were very heavy, and made of parts which were in themselves fragile, so the very existence of a ride like the Gondola is an indication of how skilful the showmen were. You see I would have thought that as time passed and the ride had got older and other people had scrapped theirs, that Percy Cole would have become more careless and abandoned the difficult routine jobs. This is what happened to the engines, some of them were in a terrible condition in the 'forties because some of the showmen let them run down, just as the railways did when the steam train was on the way out. They knew that the old technology was going and that there was something coming to replace it. Lots of the old drivers had died and the newer ones who hadn't grown up with the engines didn't give them nearly so much care. For the latter part of the time when the showman's engines were in use, they weren't half so clean or ornate as they had been in the past, so it's all the more remarkable how the Coles kept this machine as well as they did. After it was built here we had to restore the organ, but that's all. The track and the decoration is perfect. Showmen have a different view of the world to most of us. I've seen them take care of a single flat piece of painted wood from the simplest stall for years, so that in the end it has a shine and patina on it like the best furniture.

We had bought the ride in 1977, built it up in 1978 and had it

'The Gondola Switchback arriving at Thursford. This is one of the packing trucks that may have originally gone by rail between fairs.'

running by 1979. It's very popular especially with the older people, though of course we get lots of school parties here. When the schools are open there are bus loads from all over the Midlands and East Anglia. I suppose we're seen as having an educational function. Most of the children are under eleven, and they ride on the gondolas shouting at the tops of their voices, and have a hell of a time being educated here: 'Faster! Faster! Come on mate, put some more coal on!' Many of the older people are nostalgic. There was one old girl here nearly every day recently, and each time she came I helped her on to the ride. I asked her once if she minded. 'No,' she said, 'I am eighty-three after all.' 'Well you don't look it,' I said. There was another old girl standing next to her who I could see was going to say something. 'What about me,' she said, 'I'm ninety-two!' So I helped them both on to the ride and away they went. I should think that there's hardly a day goes by when we don't have people in their sixties, seventies and eighties on that machine, because it's exciting but slow and gentle. There aren't many in that age group who haven't ridden on something very similar to it in their younger days. Most working-class and lots of middle-class people went to the fairground years ago, before television trapped us. There was nowhere else to go except the seaside; our visitors remember their youth as I do myself, and more often than not they ride for hours here. Sometimes two-thirds of the passengers are elderly. I don't think that they could get on to the gallopers because it's difficult to climb on a horse, whereas it's easy to get in the cars on the gondolas, like sitting in an armchair. They can't fall out, the thing doesn't go that fast and the organ takes their minds back. There's a lot of excitement though; with the sound and the glamour they really feel that they're going somewhere. Everyone who goes on it has a good time. It makes you think. Most elderly people sit around on benches, not looking too happy, and yet here they become like silly children again. It must mean something. They all thoroughly enjoy themselves and talk about it for ages, what they all used to do and how they used to do it.

The gondolas are easy for us to drive because we use an electric motor with an old tram starter on it to make an equivalent for the slow start of a steam-driven ride. If we ran the centre engine itself the pressure would build up in the cylinders, push out the pistons and gradually increase the speed of the ride. Electrical power is either on or off, and a sudden surge of power could break something on a fairground ride, so you have to find a way to apply the power in stages. The tram starter allows you to do this, and it's easier because the current is direct, and as you move the handle from one notch to another the speed increases. It's not quite as smooth as steam would be but it isn't bad and it hasn't given us any trouble. I got the idea from the showmen who use the same thing on the modern rides. You throw the switch to full out and then pull it back a few notches so that the start is easy and slow with a gradual acceleration.

The centre is very stable so we have no worries about that. The ride is a beautiful piece of machinery. Although I'd like to get the old steam centre engine back, electricity is more practical for our circumstances. Mondays and Saturdays are not such busy days for us. We rely a lot on holidaymakers and on those days they are often going home again or just arriving, so there might only be a few local people there. The gondolas will hold sixty and if there are only two hundred people in the museum it's worth opening, but only for a couple of rides. To steam up an engine for two 3- or 4-minute rides would hardly be worth the effort, because you'd be mucking about for maybe 2 hours to do it. All we have to do now is start up the old generator, and that's that, there's no soot or ash to clear up which would give us problems indoors. It isn't like being in the open. We'd have to lay on water, put a chimney through the roof and all that kind of thing. Once, when some television people were here, we drove a ride from *Victory*, just for fun and to see how it looked. It would be similar to the way the showmen used to drive the scenics, we thought, so we used a direct current to the ride from the generators on the steam engine. What a sight it was! It really went well. A lot of people thought it wouldn't work but it drove it all right. The mechanics of both *Victory* and the ride were in as good a working order as they were sixty years before. There was no hesitation in the machinery.

At the time we didn't have a diesel generator capable of driving it and we couldn't use the mains. I was worried because the TV people were coming expecting to see it working, and I was thinking of contacting one of the showmen to hire a generator. I knew that they had pulled in for the winter and wouldn't be using any themselves. Johnny Cole was here then and said straight away, 'Why? What do you want to do that for? Steam the engine up.' It was so obvious. Here we were in a shed full of showman's engines looking for a generator. It made me laugh when I realised what I was doing. I was still a bit doubtful though, wondering if the engine would be up to the job. 'Of course it'll drive it. What do you think it was made for?' Johnny Cole seemed very confident and so Bill Jeans steamed up the engine so that the chimney was just outside the door. Because he was outside he couldn't see what was happening in the shed. He had only just started the engine and came in to see if it was working. He was surprised. The engine was going round like the clappers. He said it quite shook him, because he hadn't realised that it had started, even though he's quite a good engine driver and he'd known exactly the right speed for the job. It was unbelievable for all of us. I suppose that the last job *Victory* did was to drive the lights or dodgems on a fairground in the 'thirties, and there it was, humming away, glowing with light and sending the old ride round like a top. We had done it

'From left to right: Dick Joice, Tim Blythe who restored the Gavioli organ, Bill Jeans my friend and expert driver, Bob Ince who restored the Wurlitzer and the Marenghi, John Cole who built up the ride, Billy Barber an excellent engineer, and lastly, myself. Behind us is the Gondola ride.'

without thinking of it or planning it, but it seemed like the coming together of all those years of searching. It was as I had wanted it to be, like the old days but alive now.

Even now I never get fed up with going in there; no one will have any idea, only myself, what it does to me. I remember all the organs and engines and fairs I have seen. Lots of the older people come up to me, because I am always there, I'm in their age group and they know me. They talk to me. There were two here only yesterday and one said, 'Do you know, this is the third time I've been here this year. I can't keep away from this. . . .'

CHAPTER 7

A DESCRIPTIVE CATALOGUE

The barn where I began the collection so many years ago has been extended to about 2,000 square feet. There are over 40 engines, 9 large organs, the Wurlitzer, a working steam train and many other smaller things such as decorative work from the old fairs and so on. The collection is now a trust and all the exhibits will stay together in the future at Thursford. The backgrounds and histories of them all vary, but this is something of what I have been able to discover over the years.

Traction engines provided the power for the agricultural industry of Great Britain for the better part of a hundred years, doing threshing, ploughing, baling and other similar jobs. In 1839, the Royal Agricultural Society showed portable engines at Oxford in combination with threshing gear. At first many farmers were suspicious of these new-fangled machines, and foresaw all kinds of disasters, fires, explosions, runaways and the like. You would have thought that the whole of the population was in danger of being squashed flat to read some of the things they said, but over the years the engines developed as useful farm equipment. Steam ploughing had been attempted as early as 1836, and by 1841 Clayton & Shuttleworth were successfully making portable engines. These were not yet the self-moving engines but were towed from farm to farm by the horses.

John Fowler was typical of the inventors of the period, who saw the potential use for steam especially in undeveloped areas. The starvation in Ireland in 1846 and '47 was caused partly by badly drained fields which gave poor crops. Fowler became involved with the problem and began to think about ways in which the fields could be better drained to allow decent crops to grow. He came up with the idea of the 'Mole Drain'. What he hoped for was that the bogs would be turned into useful farm land by the application of the steam engine, and his efforts were almost on the scale of land reclamation. The 'mole' was simply a heavy metal blade which was dragged through the field at a depth of about 2ft, pulled on a cable attached to a steam engine. In a clay soil the blade made a tunnel beneath the surface which carried water off the land. This was easier and cheaper than laying pipes, and the drains were effective for years. In some cases the drains have given twenty years of use from one draining. The bullet-shaped tip of the 'mole' pulled the earth apart and left a tunnel behind it. The idea was brilliantly simple and used the natural qualities of earth, but it was totally dependent upon the power that steam could generate. In early experiments, horses pulled the blade back across the field before the next cut was made, then later two engines were used at either end of the field so that cuts could be made in both directions. Sometimes an engine would tow the blade directly behind it like a plough. Horses wouldn't have been strong enough on their own to pull the weight of the blade through the soil, and so you can see how new things became possible in farming. Previously useless land could now be worked because of even this small adaption to the engine. In 1850 John Fowler layed a drain for the Royal Agricultural Society to demonstrate the method, and six years later he ploughed an acre in one hour in a field between Ipswich and Felixstowe. At the time horses were much cheaper, but he had made his point. In the early 1860s he received an order for 150 engines to help make the Suez Canal, which must be one of the biggest 'drains' ever cut. Fowler was very clear about the value of steam, and the whole of the agricultural life of the country came to depend upon people like him, Clayton & Shuttleworth, Thomas Aveling and the others.

Engines were on show at the Great Exhibition of 1851, and by this time had been tested with loads of 50 tons. When the self-moving engine had first appeared it had sometimes travelled on the roads with a horse in shafts attached to the steering mechanism. People said that the engines frightened the horses, and this was proof that they didn't. Garretts, Claytons and Avelings all made self-movers and made several adaptations to the steering. In 1856 Burrell made his first heavy-duty steam road haulage engine. Even at the turn of the century, Burrells could still say that they were selling engines which had remained basically unchanged since the early days, and they were exporting all over the world, to Russia, Peru, France, Venezuela and many other countries. All kinds of industries came to rely on steam, from farmers to brickmakers and blacksmiths to weavers, and some continued to rely on it until the 1960s.

Garretts made the first threshing engines, and made a wide range of attachments for their machines. Thomas Aveling is credited with the first self-moving engine, and with the invention of the chain and roller steering, which enabled one man to both drive and steer, instead of having an extra man to sit up front with a directly geared steering wheel. He produced therefore one of the first recognisable traction engines, and was one of the first to make road vehicles and steam rollers, for which Avelings became so famous that their name was virtually synonymous with them.

I like to think of these small engineering companies scattered throughout East Anglia—Clayton & Shuttleworth in Lincoln, Burrell in Thetford, Garrett in Leiston, all of them employing skilled craftsmen, ordinary men who produced such marvels. I think that half the beauty of these machines is that their humanity shows. Each engine is different, not only to look at, but to drive and operate. The steam engine driver was as sensitive about the engine as a musician is about his instrument. You came to know the engine closely and to understand all its quirks and idiosyncrasies. Even the simplest of levers has a special shape and balance. If you can drive one motor car you can more or less drive any other, one Ford is pretty much the same as the next, but these engines were made as individuals for individual drivers who had specified different capacities and styles. What I am saying is that all this shows clearly in the engines themselves, and I am sure that this is a good part of what we find so wonderful now. The engines demanded something of you. They weren't passive machines, but they weren't intimidating either. They told you things about themselves and the way they were working by the sounds they made, and what sounds they were! I am sure that if you blindfolded a good engine driver he could have told you which was his engine by the sound or the touch of it. The variations were very subtle, but they were there to be read by a good man. You can see most of the works too.

There's not much that's hidden, and so they were relatively easy to maintain and clean. These are the basic working vehicles and the best from a long line of development, and I'm glad that they are here.

The Showman's Engines
The four Burrell showman's engines were the main power source for all the shows and rides owned by the Thurston family between 1905 and the late 1930s. They are classics of their kind, and there is not a set like them anywhere in the world. They are probably in as good a condition as they ever were; we've cleaned and re-made them where necessary as I've described, repainted them in their original colours, and tried to do every job as well as it would have been done at Burrell's factory, or on the fair.

The weight and mass of them is impressive, and they deserve the attention they have received. They are something grand, something special. I love the way that every detail has been made to the limits of the skill and knowledge of the period. I love the exposed machinery, or even the way that the nuts and bolts are cut to make regular patterns on the surface. I think that they knew at Burrells that these engines were as much pieces of entertainment for looking at, as they were working machines. The engines had to be spectacular and suit the pace and glamour of the fairs. I suppose that Burrells also knew that the audience would be made up of country people, engine drivers and agricultural workers who used steam engines themselves and who would be on the look out for details and perfection. Any of these engines, all lit up and working on a Saturday night, was an engine driver's dream. You had to stand next to them to see how big they were, and even then you didn't believe it. When they came up for sale in the breakers' yards in the 1940s, to me it was as though the crown jewels were being sold for scrap, and pebbles were worth more than diamonds. It seemed that the world had been turned inside out, and I would have bought them with my last pennies if I had had to.

Burrells of Thetford came to specialise in showman's engines. It is said that whenever one was completed and driven out of the factory gates, all the town came out to see it leave. There would be flowers and cheering at the sight of it, and everyone who had had anything to do with the construction of it would have come out for the occasion. It was an important event for the community. Engines took time to build in the one place, and everybody who worked in the factory had a chance to see the engine completed, and to see the whole process from beginning to end. I think that you can sense this simply by looking at the engines, and seeing how every detail has been treated with importance.

Of course, by the beginning of the century Burrells had already had a lot of experience in making steam engines of all kinds. Charles Burrell was experimenting with steam ploughs by 1853, and made many of the early portable engines. These were the steam power units from which traction engines developed, and they were pulled from farm to farm by horses. In the course of time Burrell came to make the fully fitted traction engine with road springs, belly tank and three speeds, and it was from this evolution and knowledge that the showman's engine came to be designed. The showman's engine is a farmyard engine in its best clothes, with all the buttons polished and shining.

Like every successful manufacturer of fairground equipment, Burrell obviously worked closely with the showmen for whom he was designing. Several inventions took place on the fairground which were directly linked to the power that the engines could generate. The scenics and switchbacks obviously depended upon steam to move from place to place, and upon the electricity for lights or power that the engines could produce when they were stationary at the fairs. The cranes on the scenic engines helped lift the cars from the trucks to the ride, and were a key part of the building and dismantling. All the power and weight of the engines was needed as the rides and shows became more elaborate, and more dependent upon electricity for their effects. When the bioscopes appeared in the late 1890s, the engines also played an important role. If you look closely at any photograph of a bioscope show you can usually see the wheels or the chimney of an engine that has been built into it peeping through the decoration. I think that one of the first cinema shows took place in London Polytechnic in 1896, and since it was more difficult then for people to travel, the cinemas themselves travelled with the fairs to the towns and villages. It was natural I suppose, because people were already used to going to the fair to see the shows, and the menageries were the only places on the fair with enough space to show films. Many of the earliest films were made by the showmen themselves in their own home towns, and starred the local lads and lasses. Before electrical projection, light was produced from a mixture of hydrogen and oxygen on a lime cone, and naphtha flare lamps were outside the booths. Then when the engines and generators made electricity easily available, the whole thing took off in a big way. There was an excess of light and sound from the organs, and the engines came into their own. The shows became larger, the organs more powerful, and the decorations richer. The engines were as much a part of the show as the dancing girls who were always on the front. The great period of the showman's engine was that of the bioscope show and the scenic ride from about 1900 to 1930.

By 1900 the engine on the fair had appeared in a form that we would recognise, with its twisted brass, canopy and all the fittings. All over the country they brought the first sight of moving pictures to thousands of people. I have described how I remember it all, and I am sure that it is the same for many other people, some of whom are older than myself and saw the very early years.

Diesel finally put the steam engines out of business. Lorries were faster of course, and you could get in any lorry and start it up immediately, whereas an engine needed two hours work before you could think of making a journey. Imagine working all night and then having no sleep because you had 200 miles to go and the engine wasn't even steamed up yet. A maximum speed, with the loads, might only be about 5mph, and every inch of the way would need concentration because of the weight, conditions and steam pressure. A wet, hard road with an incline could spell disaster, and there are enough photographs of accidents to prove it. Burrell tried all sorts of metal, wooden and rubber additions to the wheels, and some of them worked to a degree, but there was always a chance of something falling or slipping at the wrong time.

Showmen also came in for some of the tight regulations of local authorities, perhaps more than any other engine driver did, because they needed to travel regularly across long distances, and had to go over several county boundaries. As I discovered on my London journey, water could be a big problem, and it was worse for showmen because they often travelled by night. Still, I think that the sight of the engine and the loads on the outskirts of the towns is something that many of us miss. On occasions an engine would be pulling up to eight trucks, and that was a real advertisement for the fair. Messages would go from village to village that they were on their way, and it seemed that they had come out of nowhere, from the other side of England which was a world away.

Charles Thurston bought the first of his bioscope shows in 1901, and this was powered by *Alexandra*. The show was built on to two wagons and had a Gavioli organ. By 1905 the firm had more equipment including Flying Pigs and Waltzing Balloons, and needed another engine, so *King Edward VII* was ordered and used mostly with the bioscope show. In 1908 Thurstons bought their 'Great Show' from Orton & Spooner Ltd. It had a 120-key Marenghi, a system of lights which operated in time with the organ, and it travelled until 1914. *Unity* arrived on the scene in 1910, and finally *Victory* came to Lynn Mart in 1920 as I've described. *King Edward VII* was altered and then rebuilt to its present size. That might seem a big job to any of us, but the showmen were always changing their equipment, and in times of rapid change it might happen every year. Even now it is thought nothing to cut lorries in half to extend them if more power or more space is needed, and you can see real feats of engineering skill on a fair.

Other important features on *Victory* and *King Edward VII* are the lengths of steel cable which were used to pull trucks off waterlogged ground. Quite often the venue for the fair would be the village green, or a field on the edge of town, and when the weather was bad the field would turn into a bog overnight. Sometimes the whole fair was ruined, and the showmen had built up and opened for nothing, because no one would make the trip across a marsh to spend their money. These cables are still an essential part of fairground life even now. It is important for the showmen to leave the surface of the ground undamaged, and if a truck should get stuck the easiest way to move it is to place the engine or lorry on the solid road and haul the embedded vehicle out by winch and cable. In the mid- and late 1940s, showman's engines were much in demand for demolishing bomb-damaged buildings in London. They could pull down dangerous factories safely and there was nothing else available which had the power and weight or could be adapted to the situation. There was no room for explosives, and lorries were too light or too long for the job. You can see that *Victory*, with its lifting gear, generator and winch was useful in all weathers and for all kinds of emergencies, as well as being a big part of the show. The engine weighs some 17 tons, could haul up to 45 tons and more, and the crane could move 30cwt at a time.

Between 1920 and 1930 the engines all pulled, drove or lit the different rides and shows of the Thurston family. A set of Chairoplanes was bought, operated and sold within three years as the turnover of rides was rapid, depending upon which one was taking money. There was the fire which destroyed the dragon cars on the scenic, and many other minor changes happened which meant different jobs for the engines, such as driving, producing electricity or pulling loads so that rides could open on time and blaze with light. By 1926 a set of Jolly Tubes was being transported on a FWD lorry, and by 1929 two more lorries had been bought to replace a small Burrell and a Garrett. A Swirl, the first of the modern rides had been bought at the same time and was powered by *Alexandra* for a short time, but the end of the steam age had already begun. In 1930 the large Peacock ride, which I remember so well, stayed in the yard and a set of dodgems replaced it at Lynn Mart, this time driven by *King Edward VII*. It was not until much later that the two old steam rides were sold to Butlins, but they were phased out in the 'thirties. In fact the smaller of the steam rides, called the 'Little Machine', made its last appearance in 1930 at the Norwich Easter Fair.

Noah's Arks, Waltzers and Swirls took the place of the scenics, though some of the newer rides were still driven by steam for a while. In 1935 a new Lakin-built Noah's Ark was driven by *Alexandra* at Kettering Feast. By 1937 *King Edward VII* stayed in the yard, and in 1946 *Alexandra*, the oldest engine, was the only one still in use. It was finally replaced that year by a Diamond T lorry, and in December of the following year *Victory*, *Unity* and *Alexandra* came to Thursford. *Victory* had made its last journey in 1939, from Oxford to Norwich, covering 110 miles in one day. Oxford Fair had been cancelled because of the outbreak of the war, and so the loads had been taken back to the yard by the engine for the last time. It wasn't until 1960 that *King Edward VII* came to Thursford and we could start to restore them all together. I don't really feel that they have stopped work, because they are still drawing the crowds, and they are after all only 20 miles away from their original winter quarters. *Victory* was the first engine to be fully restored, only twelve years after its sale to the breakers.

The Garrett engine *Medina* is a complete contrast to the Burrells. They are massive showman's engines, and *Medina* is only half their size and weight. Everything on the engine is scaled down, so that you

St Giles Fair, Oxford, in 1901. Thurston's three rides may be seen on the left. (*H. W. Taunt, William Keating Collection*)

would almost say that it is a pretty engine. It was built in Leiston, Suffolk, by Garretts in their own factory there, and numbered 33902. It has all the standard equipment that you would expect to find on a full-sized showman's engine, with two speeds, and is based on the design for an ordinary road engine that Garretts made at that time. Because it isn't so vast you can see how everything works from the ground, and people like to peer into the cab to look at the dials and knobs. It doesn't tower over you like the others do, so you can get in close and have a good look.

Weight restrictions were always changing from one local authority to the next in the period when *Medina* was working, and the showmen could never be sure what regulations they would be required to meet. *Medina* was weighed at 6.5 tons, probably to avoid a restriction of 7 tons. Some manufacturers used to weigh their engines whilst they were still incomplete, to avoid tolls or penalties and to allow access through as many counties as possible. From their beginnings engines had been disliked by many farmers because the smallest sparks could set light to a haystack, though they rarely did. Local authorities could close bridges at short notice, or enforce detours or impose extreme payment at the tolls. Separate licences were often required for steam vehicles for each different county, and this was especially difficult for showmen. People complained about engines frightening the horses, or the coal or ash burning the green. Time was when these engines, now so admired, were considered the scourge of civilization. I know of one showman who recently refused the offer of a nostalgic trip to see one, because he said that all they reminded him of was work and dirt.

In normal use *Medina* could pull some 12 tons, travel 12 miles between stops for water, and 21 miles before stopping for coal. Notice the acetylene lamps at the front, and imagine driving in winter and at night under the kind of restrictions that were operating then. Showmen's drivers were amongst the most skilful of all, because they had to develop a range of skills unknown to local drivers, and travel over all kinds of countryside. They could travel at speed over the flat Norfolk landscape, and negotiate the bends and hills of the West Country, all with the expensive and heavy loads behind them. Driving was more than a job which had to be done between certain hours. It was a life from which there was no release. Journeys extended far into the night, or began as dawn was breaking, and at either end was the building and dismantling which had to be done whatever the weather. The engines and the drivers were the heart of the fair.

The Organs

The MARENGHI is a magnificent and beautiful organ. It has a lot of style, and belongs very much to its period. It is thought to have been built in 1905 in Paris, and in 1910 was awarded the Grand Prix at the Brussels World Fair. It has all the characteristics of the Paris of the turn of the century, and was probably used in a dance hall before it was exported to Great Britain. Chipperfields owned it at first, then it was sold to the Barry family who showed it at the Bellevue Park, Belfast. It is probably the only one of its kind in existence which is a full pipe organ. The colours are marvellous and the horses at the top and the girl are impressive. Then the dragons, the head of Bacchus and the four paintings of the seasons are worth looking at too. None of our restorers would touch the pictures because they said they were so good. What I like about the whole front is the way that there are so many different styles brought together, which don't jar on each other at all. The organ has a lovely light, soft feel about it. The shape is nice, and the columns which divide the front have lots of character in them, which gives the design a rhythm. The shells at the top are pretty, and if you look at the whole front from a distance you see that it is like a sea shell in shape and colour. You can imagine that the image of the girl and the horses has been made from a memory of the patterns of the surf or the crest of a wave which an artist noticed somewhere on the shore.

We are just starting a new restoration of the organ, stripping the whole thing, and rebuilding the pipes and mechanisms so that it will play as it was intended that it should. We can never stop working on the things we have here, and we are never satisfied with them. Because most of them are working machines, there will always be a certain number of repairs which need doing. We have tried to use all the old materials wherever possible and to keep to the original in all details, because we want to do the job properly. Some of the leather in the pipes has worn so badly over the years that the instrument wasn't sounding well and the whole process of rebuilding will probably take about eighteen months from start to finish. Bob Ince, who restored the Wurlitzer, learnt a lot from that which he says is useful on this much older organ, though for an instrument of its age it is in remarkably good condition. A few pipes were blocked so that they would play on some days and not on others, and we discovered one or two that probably hadn't played for years.

We also found that the organ had probably been enlarged at some time from a 75-key instrument, because the baritone and trombone chant pipes are not original. Also Bob noticed a date on the bellows, 12 April 1911, whereas the front does seem to date from 1905. The craftsmen who worked on the organ originally have left their marks all over it. One of the three people who worked on the bellows was called Jerome; he has inscribed his name there and someone else has written his nickname.

Charles Marenghi was one of the most famous of those who had worked for Gavioli and then set up in business for himself. He left shortly after Gavioli's financial crisis at the beginning of this century, and manufactured 89-, 92-, 94- and 98-key instruments, sometimes by completing work which Gavioli had started. From 1907 fully chromatic keys became available and were produced by all the leading manufacturers, including Limonaire and Chiappa & Sons in London. Using some of Gavioli's ideas, and introducing more of his own, Marenghi became successful and made several larger organs of over a hundred keys. The figures on the front became something of a Marenghi speciality, and he was the first to experiment with light shows. The organ fronts had lights which changed with the sounds, and would be operated by the same perforated books which produced the music. Competition was fierce and Marenghi knew that the organs had to look good as well as sound good. The showmen of Great Britain were certainly impressed with his work and showed it as much as possible on all the rides and displays. A Marenghi was a money-spinner. Among those showmen who used Marenghis were President Kemp on his travelling theatres, the 'Theatre Unique' and the 'Palace of Light', often seen at Nottingham Goose Fair in the early 1900s, Anderton & Rowland, Marshall Hill on a Scenic Railway, Relph and Pedley on their shows, and one was even used to draw crowds to a travelling film show called 'The Heavyweight Championship of the World'. The façades of the Marenghis seemed to suit the kind of decoration which was being done at the same time on the fairs elsewhere, and the bright sound was the one which showmen were seeking because it carried well over the noise of the crowds.

The MORTIER 112-key dance organ is a complete contrast to the Marenghi. It was made in 1938, weighs 4½ tons, and is typical of the kind of work for which the firm became famous. Some 1,400 instruments were made between 1890 and 1950, when I understand the firm closed. The front is darker in tone and richer than the pinks and pastels of the Marenghi. It is full of the dense kind of decoration which you might have found in the cinemas of the 1930s. Every space is filled with clusters of shapes, dots, stripes, curls or leaf patterns, so that the effect is one of loudness and vigour rather than grace. Every shape actually jars with the next one and it doesn't really matter because the organ was for entertainment in a jazz age, and was designed to make as much impact as possible. Earlier Mortier organs were more like the Marenghi, with separate carved figures and a more elegant decorative style. Most of the firm's organs stayed in Belgium, and they didn't export their work as the other manufacturers did, to far distant places in the world.

In many ways Mortiers were architects of the organ. Some of their instruments were made in the shape of palaces or temples, and were huge in size. The firm started almost by accident. Theophile Mortier was a restaurateur who had a Gavioli in the shop which he sold to a customer, and then replaced it with another. This too was sold, and Mortier soon found himself in the business of selling organs full-time. Before long a workshop was needed, and by 1908 he was making repairs to organs with a team of skilled men. The story is that things became complicated because Gavioli was giving technical advice on the condition that Mortier didn't use the information to make organs under his own name, and that is precisely what Mortier began to do. Now whether or not the details are exactly true no one can be sure, but, so the story goes, after a long and drawn out court case it was decided that Mortier could build his own organ fronts, provided that he ordered a certain number of organs each year from Gavioli. It seems that Mortier ordered too many, and the Italian firm couldn't meet the orders, so that the court's conditions were void, and Mortier went into business on his own. By the end of the First World War Mortiers were making a new organ every two or three weeks.

The firm had a team of skilled men working for them, some of whom had worked for Gavioli and were familiar with his ideas. Mortier experimented with new instrumentation, and added jazz flutes, saxophones and Hammond organs which played perfectly in the larger framework. One of their theatre organs was converted into a church organ, and all kinds of adaptations were considered. The early models were enormous creations in the baroque style. One famous one was called the 'Taj Mahal' and was 20ft high with sculptured figures and columns. Others were made in a Turkish style, or were fitted with bronze bells, but by 1930 the patterns had changed into something like the kind of organ we have here now. The sound is very powerful, and is much like a modern dance orchestra, so that you often find that someone takes it into their head to cavort about while it is playing.

The CARL FREI is another of my favourites. It is a bit of a mixture to look at and it certainly doesn't have the overall unity of style that the Marenghi or the Mortier have, but it is a good organ built on to one trailer so that it is easy to move around. The trailer also acts as a kind of frame for the picture of the front and gives it something of the appearance of a puppet theatre. It was made as a 100-key organ originally, and was in a bad way when it was found in the 1960s before they rebuilt it for me in the style I wanted. It has a very good bass sound and can store half an hour's worth of book music at a time.

The history of the Carl Frei Company begins with the birth of the founder in Waldkirch, Germany, in 1884. By the time he was a teenager he was writing and arranging music and had apprenticeships at both the Bruder Company and Gavioli. He also worked for Mortier for a short time before setting up his own business. Soon after the First World War he had begun a venture in Holland, making street organs, then the Second World War forced closure and a return to the home town where he had arranged music for the local band in his teens. Since then the firm has become famous, and is continued by the family now. They have kept to the older style of decoration and have produced rococo façades with fully carved figures, perhaps because they stayed close to the traditional roots and to the geographical location they knew.

The WELLERHAUS is a small and compact organ, but a very powerful instrument. The top folds up to act as a sounding board, which makes it a very useful thing to have on a fairground or on a noisy street. It can be transported easily because it is so small, and then opened up quickly to belt out a good noise.

The HOOGHUYS was built in Belgium in 1900 as a fairground organ, and was used for many years by Albert Bequart's family. Unlike some other firms in Belgium, Hooghuys made instruments that were bright and fast, rather than soft voiced. This one has a glockenspiel which gives the whole sound a silver tone, and the prettiness of the painted front with its pastel shades and delicate drawing follows from the lightness of the sound.

Organs have their origins in all sorts of things. The old woodcuts of medieval fairs show acrobats and jugglers, freaks and sword swallowers, all of whom were accompanied by musical instruments of some kind, including drums, bells, surprise sounds, explosions, flutes and rude noises. Even as late as the beginning of this century bands of musicians were common on the show fronts such as Sedgwicks' Menagerie with its large brass section. So organs on the fair simply took over the job of making the loud attractive music that drew a crowd and kept their interest and attention. Most organs are based on early wind instruments, and of course there was the long existing tradition of church organs, which had created generations of skilled craftsmen. Even some of the decoration on the fairs reminds me of churches. There are the angles for instance on the fronts of the shows, some of which look exactly like the ones you see on altars or on the ceilings of some churches. Then some of the monsters too look like gargoyles that you can find on religious buildings all over Europe. Whatever their origins the organs are compelling entertainers which still seem to have a strong effect on everyone who comes here.

The WURLITZER is one of the largest Wurlitzers ever seen in Europe, and was built in 1931–2 by the Rudolph Wurlitzer Company in New York for the cinema in the Headrow in Leeds. There are 1,339 pipes ranging from 16ft to ½in in length. Because they were originally in two rooms on either side of the screen, we had to go the whole way and have the two rooms specially built here at Thursford, separated from the main hall by swell shutters which open and close as a volume control of the organ. The organ played to 3,500 people in Leeds and we have tried to make the acoustics suit the large sound. The organ is a monster. A discus blower is driven by a 15hp motor and supplies air at some 1,500 cubic feet per minute, at 1lb per square inch. Each of the organists who come here seem to find something new about the instrument. It is a machine, but the effects which can be made upon it vary from the comic to the mysterious, from the 'horse trot' to the orchestral sound.

The original Rudolph Wurlitzer went from Germany to America in 1856 with £350, and began selling woodwind instruments in Cincinatti. He moved to Chicago in 1865, and by 1890 the company was thriving by making and selling hand played instruments. Rudolph had the commercial notion of producing coin operated musical boxes which were also very successful, and the company expanded from there. Although most people would know the name 'Wurlitzer' from their juke boxes or theatre organs, the company made fairground organs, or 'Band Organs' as they were known in America, for many years, and there are three heroes in the story of their making.

If Rudolph Wurlitzer was the first, Eugense Dekleist was the second. In 1893 he had started 'The North Tonnawanda Barrel Organ Works'

157

in New York. Four years later he began a working arrangement with the Wurlitzer Company, and soon Wurlitzer was the sole agent, then virtually the sole manufacturer of his instruments. Before 1901 most of the firm's organs were to be heard in skating rinks, and it wasn't until 1920 that fairs became important. The 1912 catalogue boasted:

> Our perforated paper roll military band organs furnish better music to skate by than any musicians, and after the first cost of the organ your music costs you nothing, save the small expense of a few new music rolls occasionally.

Wurlitzer was responsible for one very important invention, the use of paraffin-soaked paper for the music. Ordinary paper distorted when it became damp, whereas the 'Weather Proofed Music Hall Rolls revolutionised band organ construction . . . cut on specially treated paper'. The rolls were extremely strong and durable, made to stand long use and changes of temperature. All kinds of musical sounds were attempted, from trumpets to violins, including one instrument called the 'Paganini', which represented a small orchestra in American cinemas and entertained the audience before and during the films.

'Meanwhile back in England', as the films themselves might say, was the third hero in the story of the Wurlitzer. In many ways he is the most interesting of the three, because he was a man of invention and curiosity, neither of which did him much good. He was a telephone engineer, part-time organ builder and musician called Robert Hope-Jones. He was experimenting with all kinds of ideas and ways for improving the sound of organs with electricity. At seventeen he had been apprenticed to Lairds the shipbuilders, and moved from there to become a chief electrician with the Lancashire and Cheshire Telephone Company. He improved the telephone and also invented a fog warning device largely as a result of his experimental work on electric organs. No wonder the Wurlitzer came to have such power. Hope-Jones began his organ business in England, then moved to the USA in 1903 with some of his workmen and set up there. He probably wasn't a very good business man, and his firm was in a definite trough when, quite by chance, some of the directors of the Wurlitzer Company heard a concert by one of Jones' organs in the Ocean Grove, New York. By 1910 they had bought all the patents and workshops, and given Hope-Jones a job on their staff. You would have thought that at last the man's troubles were over, but it wasn't so. All his life he had been obsessional about organs. There are photos of him playing at a very early stage of his career, and he was so convinced that there were always new sounds to be discovered that he couldn't leave a good idea alone. He was continually tinkering with the organs he built, trying for just a bit more tone, vibrato or volume. In the end the part of the Wurlitzer Company that he ran began to lose money, and the directors of the firm barred him from the factory. Although they continued to pay him a fee, he was distraught and killed himself in September 1914.

This is how the Wurlitzer–Hope-Jones orchestra, or what we know as the Wurlitzer, came into being, developed from the skills of a telephone engineer, an instrument seller from Germany and an immigrant entrepreneur, for a booming American entertainment market. By 1920 some 2,200 organs had been built. Early in the 1920s they had begun to arrive in the cinemas in Great Britain, and good organists made them popular there and on the radio. The BBC broadcast many concerts from 1926, and continued with them for the next twenty-five years, so that the names of the musicians became household words: Reginald Dixon and Sandy Macpherson were two of the best. Talking films merely enhanced the fame of the organs. The image of the cinema organ rising through the floor is familiar to most people, and by the 1930s the organs were in their heyday. The Wurlitzer at Thursford comes from that great period and is thought by some writers to be one of the finest organs ever to have been made by the company. The Paramount organisation bought three specially for their main cinemas in Leeds, Manchester and Newcastle. Most of the better organists of the time played there, and came from all over the world.

The console is white with gold lining, about 6ft across, and from there all the pipes in the two rooms beyond the dampers are controlled. You can see why they were so popular. There is a great mystery and thrill attached to the sound, and I always feel a tingle in my spine as the first few notes are played.

The Gondola Switchback

The Gondola switchback was first owned by George Aspland who bought it new from Savage & Company in the 1890s and was one of the most fascinating of showmen. Ralph Howden-Aspland has chatted to me for hours about him, and so I feel that I know a lot about the inside story of the ride. Ralph is seventy himself and has worked hard to keep the family history intact, so that most of the references you can find in books now about the Asplands have come from him.

George Aspland was in business with his brother-in-law, Ben Howden. Ralph's father was Ben's eldest son, but he grew up and lived with George because his own family, with three older sisters, was too big for the wagon in which they travelled. Because of this he was christened Howden Aspland, which became his own family name. Ralph lives in Boston where the family settled in the early part of the century, and has kept all the photos and articles in the newspapers which deal with events surrounding the ride. It's difficult to know where to begin; perhaps the best place is with the original George Aspland himself.

He was born in 1836 in Holbeach in Lincolnshire. His father was a joiner, and his mother died when he was only four years old. He was out to work early in life and went from errand boy to a job on the land, on a threshing machine. Maybe the hardness of the work, which I knew well too, prompted him to begin to think of other ways to make a living, or it may have been a natural playful spirit and a feeling for entertainment, but he started experimenting with a home-made shooting gallery, to make sport for himself and the local lads. At first it was very primitive, with an iron target, and the range marked out by a simple rope from where you took your shot. The marks on the target were wiped out by another lad who had a pail of whitewash and a large brush, and the stories are that it was a riot on the cricket ground at Holbeach where it was first seen, so that there was as much whitewash on the throwers as there was on the targets. This gave George more confidence and he was soon travelling further afield with a properly constructed shooting gallery of the old kind. These had tubes through which you fired, proper guns and targets, and a wagon on which to carry them. I'm told that the wagon itself was a sight, piled high with pipes, guns and rope, rumbling along from place to place, but it made George a good living.

By the late 1860s he had made a photography booth to go with the range, so that you could have your photo taken with your prize or your favourite girl or boy. He did all the developing and printing himself in the booth. Within a few years he had made a few bob and bought himself an early roundabout, and also a set of bicycles, which were arranged in a circle like a roundabout so that people paid to pedal themselves round. Obviously when the ride was full it went round at a good speed, and quite often it was difficult to stop. George would end up running at the riders, shouting and waving at them to stop pedalling, but they didn't always listen. The answer to the problem was to have a steam-driven ride, so that he could stop the machine and control the speed from the centre. I don't know whether he ever got his own back by putting the engine flat out, but I wouldn't be surprised if sometimes the old pedals went round a bit faster than they should have done. I am sure that Frederick Savage, who became so famous for his fairground equipment, would have listened to George to find out about things like this, that you could only discover when the fair was open.

The forerunner of the switchback was the 'Sea-on-Land', and George Aspland had the first steam-driven set of these in 1880, opening in Halifax on 24 June. Sanger's Circus had visited Boston in May with a horse-driven version, but steam added much more pace and power to the whole thing. The Sea-on-Land's first visit to Norwich Tombland Fair was in Easter 1881, and it went from there to Great Yarmouth. That week saw one of the first Fisheries Exhibitions ever seen in the whole country, which was opened by the Prince of Wales in the Drill Hall, Norwich, to coincide with the fair. The Home Secretary was there too, and a large procession led the way past Castle Hill and the fairground. All the trucks from the fair were brought out by Ben Howden for the people to stand on to see the procession go by. I've told you how we first saw electricity on the fair, but that first visit of the Sea-on-Land brought the very first electric light to Norwich, and you can imagine the effect it had, a huge carbon lamp outside the exhibition, flickering alternately bright and dim, with a blue tint. It must have been mysterious and maybe frightening. I've seen people in my time who were worried by it, though I have seen others, lads from the villages, go up to the electric lamps on a fair, stand to one side of them, and try to blow them out, without anyone seeing them. They had very sore cheeks before they gave up.

George Aspland soon had other rides working for him, including the galloping horse roundabout called 'The West Norfolk Hunters', and eventually the Gondola switchback we have at Thursford now, which was the first set ever made. He has an important place in the history of the fairground, because he was the first with several of the major inventions that Savage & Co produced, and would have tried and tested everything, maybe adding suggestions of his own to the early models, and telling Savage how things were going so that any necessary changes could be made. For example, it was George's idea to have a loose centre circle of canvas at the apex of the top canvas cover so that strong winds could blow through the ride, rather than lifting the whole canvas and the ride with it. Though you might not think that the wind could move a roundabout weighing several tons, it has happened to my certain knowledge on several occasions, sometimes wrecking thousands of pounds worth of equipment. Asplands seem to have had a close relationship with Savage, and were also one of the first to have an electrically driven scenic.

The gondolas can be seen in their early years in some of the illustrations which Ralph has loaned to me. If you look at plate 28 you will see that the organ now in the ride at Thursford was originally in the travelling cinema that Asplands operated. When it was taken out it had to be cut down from 110 keys to 98 so that it would fit in the ride, under the driving ring. Incidentally the carved frames which used to frame the lamps on this show are now in the museum here too. Asplands had travelled with the earliest cinemas, and when George settled in 1909 in Boston, he began to open a series of cinema theatres, which continued as the family business. He lived in the Sea-on-Land Terrace which he built in 1884 from the profits of the fairs he had visited. The workshops for the wintertime repairs were behind the terrace, and it was there that the new gold leaf had been put on the sections of the ride stored there during the off-season. Much later the workshops were sold to a garage, and you can still see one of the carved wooden heads of Neptune from the Sea-on-Land, now stuck on top of the garage as a faint reminder of the early days of glory.

George Aspland died two years after settling down, on the last day of Boston Fair, and all the flags on the fairground were flown at half-mast. The showmen held a service in Asplands' Exhibition Show, and the Chaplain to the Showmen's Guild read an address to the packed theatre. Even now he is still remembered.

The photographs of the rides are interesting to me. You can see that the early switchback is basically the same as the gondolas, except that

'Asplands Mammoth Exhibition, the bioscope show with the 110-key Gavioli in about 1906. This is the same organ at present in the gondolas at Thursford.'

the earlier ride has the cars exposed to the air, each with its own separate canopy. All that happened later was that the roof was extended over the whole thing to enclose the moving centre; the cars on the switchback also had tops on them, but for decoration.

The photo of York shows the fair and the ride open in the grounds of the asylum there. The attitude to mental illness was cruder then, and on Fridays only the patients were brought round the fair handcuffed to each other and to their nurse. I'm afraid the children teased them mercilessly, and then ran away to hide on the gondolas. The grounds were 10 acres in size, and the oval fair was set out in the centre. Everyone had to pay at a turnstile to get into the ground, and there were pass-outs for anyone who wanted to go out again for fish and chips from the van parked outside. You can see that the gondolas were bigger then than they are now, with a platform which cantilevered out from the side of the machine so that more people could stand to watch or queue for a ride. The platform was packed, and watching was part of the fun, particularly if there was a new face you had noticed.

163

There were two of the gas-filled balloons you can see in the centre of the picture and for a few pence you could have a ride in the sky. Whilst one balloon was being brought back across the grounds from wherever it had landed, the other was being loaded up with passengers. One year, around the time of the photograph, it's said that two showmen, Tippler White and William Doubtfire, were in one of the local pubs, tight as newts, and had a dispute which became a bet involving a ride in the balloon. Now, they were both big men, and a little the worse for wear, so that when the balloon took off it didn't go straight up as it should have done, or in a very straight line, but over the top of the gondolas instead, knocking the chimney off as it went. You can still see the evidence if you look closely. Ralph told me that there was quite a commotion, with everyone running everywhere, shouting, whilst the two culprits rose slowly into the sky.

The gondolas were sold to Percy Cole in 1937 or '38, and prior to that Asplands had been offered £800 just for the gold leaf that was on the ride. A firm wanted to pay that just to remove the gold. They weren't interested in the ride, and £800 was a lot of money then. Several things have vanished over the years, and we will have to do all we can to restore them. The figures on the photo taken at Stamford have gone, and our top rounding boards are from a later scenic. There used to be more carved work around the driving ring which propels the cars too.

Ralph's good sense in keeping the photographs has made it possible to see the changes as they took place. For example, sometimes the gondola cars were replaced with motor cars where George Aspland thought they would be a better attraction for the crowds. The large extended arch which you can see at Thursford was made at Orton & Spooners later to make a bit of a splash at the front. We have a lot of work to do, and we're busy looking for the painters and craftsmen who have the skills and sensitivity to manage it.

'The prototype switchback made for George Aspland by Frederick Savage in about 1882. A very basic ride, but one that was to be the original for decades of other designs. George Aspland is the bowler-hatted man seated on the rail to the left of the photo.'

'York Gala in 1906 with its fair and balloon. The gondolas are the first of the large roundabouts to the right of the balloon.'

YORK GALA JUNE 21ST '06

The switchback is typical of the rides made by Savage & Co in King's Lynn between 1880 and about 1910, and was the prototype for most of them. It would have been built over a period of some $7\frac{1}{2}$ months, cost something like £13,000 and involved 600 craftsmen, and those are some of the reasons that no more are built now. It has a steam engine set lengthways on the truck in the centre of the ride which was used originally for power, driving a set of gears and the frame which is attached to the cars on the track. Savage made hundreds of such sets and they were extremely popular, the mainstay of his business.

Frederick Savage was born in 1828 and died in 1897. He was the most prominent designer of fairground and agricultural equipment in his period. The mechanics of the two kinds of machinery are very similar, and in the beginning, Savage simply arranged for the roundabouts to be pulled around by a horse in shafts, or sometimes they were cranked by hand. It was really the application of steam power though which allowed the development of the fairground that

'The gondolas at Stamford, Lincolnshire, in 1901. The figures around the outside are beautiful, and look at all the carved work in the centre. All the cars have canopies in place, and the early barrel organ is encrusted with carved figures too.'

we have nowadays. Until the early 1860s roundabouts played a relatively small part on the fair. If you look at books like Henry Morley's *Bartholomew Fair*, you will see that there were also many shows, stalls, drinking booths, acrobats, markets and such like. It seems that for centuries fairs had survived as places of trade, where things could be bought, sold or exchanged. This is how 'Nottingham Goose Fair' came to be so called. The entertainments attached themselves to the main commercial business of the event, and went hand in hand with it. The whole thing was really a glamorised market, where people went to have a good time as well as trade for a living. I've read that Norfolk had important fairs long before the Middle Ages. King's Lynn is a good example, and Blakeney on the North Norfolk coast was a link in a trade route which stretched to Russia. This is how things went on for a long time, until the Industrial Revolution put an end to it all by dramatically improving methods of transport and communication. When towns and villages began to have their own shops and centres of trade, the fairs lost what had been their main function. There was no reason for people to go to Nottingham if they could buy or sell at a good profit in their own shops, or if the trains brought the world to their door. So when Savage applied steam power to the rides he rescued the fairs and restored a purpose for their existence, because he made possible more elaborate roundabouts. The limits of a horse's strength applied on the fair as they did on the land; a horse could only pull so much, but a steam engine could really generate some power, so that you could build great big rides with lots of carvings and great big animals. This is what people came to want, and the steam also allowed the fairs to travel widely.

It was to the small towns and villages in Norfolk that some of the early inventions came. Sidney Soames brought one of the first steam roundabouts to Aylsham, not far from Thursford, in 1862. Savage probably saw it there—he was always keen on a new idea—and tried it to see what it was worth. He was trained as a blacksmith in the country and so knew all about making an unlikely object work. One of Savage's best-known inventions was the galloping horse roundabout. There were two kinds. Sometimes the horses were suspended from the top of the ride and swung out as they went faster. Most of the existing gallopers are of this kind, and Noyce's are a good example. You can see them every year at Oxford Fair. On platform gallopers the horses were attached to the lower platform of the ride, like the cars on the switchback, but they had a system of gears to make them go up and down as though they were galloping. Sometimes cockerels were used instead of horses, and on another type there was a small steam train on a track in the centre. Whatever the variations though, the gallopers and the switchback were the basic idea for most of the rides.

The gondolas were designed to be dismantled and rebuilt each week, and it's only when you see showmen doing it that you realise how clever the design is. The most important part of the job is to get everything level from the start. The centre truck has to be raised on blocks and made steady, because it is from there that the rest of the ride is built. If there was any unevenness the machine could shake itself to pieces at speed. The static frame which supports the rails on which the cars travel is built outwards from the centre, and then the cars are pulled around by a system of arms, called Swifts and Sullivans, which spread out from the top of the centre, driven directly from the engine. I thing that Savages made their last switchback somewhere around 1908, but the general pattern of the structure of rides was to remain the same right up to today.

The organ on our switchback is one of the best I have heard. Lots of people have written about it over the years. The Fairground Circle of Showland Fans used to have a magazine called the *Merry-go-Round*. Father Greville, who was the editor, had been the Secretary of the Showmen's Guild, so he knew a lot about organs, and in the spring edition of 1946 he described it as the 'finest organ in the country'. I don't know about that, but Gaviolis were certainly among the most popular and reliable of organs, and this is a beautiful one. It has lots of brass trumpets with a good clean sound, and has been well cared for over the whole of its working life. Verbeeck rebuilt it in 1926, and we've had it restored again since it has been here. The violin sounds are

'The opening of King's Lynn Mart in 1904, showing the gondolas to the right of the photograph, packed with locals trying to see the mayor performing the opening ceremony. For days the whole fair was crowded like this.' (*William Keating Collection*)

'This photograph was taken at Hull Fair in about 1906, and you can see from the placard announcing Aspland's fortieth visit that they were well established there even then. The gondola cars have been replaced with motor cars for this fair.'

marvellous, and there is an extra regulator to control the flow of air, so that long chords can be heard clearly and don't lose tone or pitch. Some of the music is original, and was made by some of the best in the business, Verbeeck, Marenghi and Varetto.

I always did like the sound of a Gavioli. The man himself had been one of the first to make organs of this kind, and most of the other manufacturers of organs had some link or other with his firm. Varetto, for example, had been a foreman there and took over part of his business in Manchester, and of course Marenghi also worked for him. Gavioli was without a doubt the best-known manufacturer of fairground organs in the nineteenth and early twentieth centuries. The origins of the firm go back to the early 1800s in Italy, before Anselme Gavioli moved to Paris. There were lots of setbacks in the early days. Customers vanished with their organs without having paid for them. There was a fire in the factory in Alsace in 1871, and then in 1901 most of the firm's money had to be put into major repairs of the buildings. It was because of these financial difficulties that Charles Marenghi left to begin his own business, taking with him several of the Gavioli craftsmen and ideas.

In 1905 the firm was still employing 300 men, and had offices scattered all over, in New York, Antwerp, Barcelona, Milan and Manchester, but it was not to last much longer. Ludovic Gavioli resigned when the managers voted to make vacuum cleaners rather than organs. Marenghi rebuilt many Gaviolis under his own name, and Limonaire and the Berni Organ Co seem to have taken over other ideas. There were many reasons for the demise of Gavioli: some say that the guarantees that they gave were too good, and that their standards proved too expensive to maintain in the face of the competition. Their 89- and 98-key instruments were very popular, and in many ways they were the Rolls-Royce of organs. The one we have here is the last of its kind, and suits the switchback perfectly.

The switchbacks and scenics vanished with the end of the steam era in about 1930. They were very expensive to buy, and the showmen's families had invested huge sums of money in them. They thought that they had bought something for their children and grandchildren to use to make their living, with perhaps a change of cars now and then. As soon as diesel was available and the new waltzers came, everything changed overnight almost. When one of the first appeared in 1929 at

Lynn Mart, most of the visitors to the fair left everything else to go and have a look. Some people blame the showmen for the loss of the old rides, but that's not really doing them justice. In the first place there wouldn't have been any old rides without them, and in the second place, what could they have done? They had their living to make, they weren't able to subsidise the rides from anywhere. Many of the machines went back to the factory because the showmen couldn't meet the payments, and I think many of them were eventually burnt. The new swirls not only took more money, they were easier to travel around because they were lighter, and the new flat style of decoration evolved to match the thrill of them, which suited the customers. Fred Fowle began painting in a bright and flamboyant manner, and the modern style of ride was complete.

Though the modern rides had a different appearance, they were all based on the ideas that Frederick Savage worked out at the end of the nineteenth century, and if you compare our switchback with a swirl you will see what I mean. There is the same underlying pattern and structure, and the main gears in the centre look very similar. In the early days of invention there had been many constructions which simply did not work. All kinds of people were trying to make rides which would be colourful and attractive, and at the same time come to pieces easily and carry passengers safely. It took ages for the gallopers to evolve to their present design, and only Savage was clever enough to think of grooves cut in the platform to regulate the outward swinging motion of the horses, or a system of cranks which gives the horses the up and down movement. He also invented the third rail on the track, which you can see on our switchback, that stopped the cars from jumping off at speed, and also the canvas stretchers between the cars which stopped anyone from falling between them. Several of these ideas were safety devices, because this had to be a major concern if only for the sake of business.

All kinds of news has traditionally travelled with the fairs. I've described the way we all saw electricity there, and the cinemas. Between 1896 and 1914 the fair was the place where films were to be seen, and the decorated fronts of the organ developed against a background of steam. There were strong European influences in the carving. Some say that foreign workmen helped with the work or the design at King's Lynn or Burton-on-Trent where most of the carving was done, but whatever the case, the influences are very strong and mixed. If you look at the cups and saucers or the furniture of the period you will see the same thing, except that there was more scope for fantasy on a fairground.

I was sad to see Savage & Co finally close in the 1970s. Though they hadn't done fairground work for years, the wooden patterns were still there and so were some of the craftsmen who had the skills. Savage himself had been a good entrepreneur and I doubt if he would have let it all go. He knew a good idea when he saw one, and the main reason for his success, I am sure, was that he always worked closely with the travelling showmen. He realised that they knew their craft well, and picked up lots of tips from them about the day-to-day running of a fair. A ride like the switchback had to fit in with the economic and family structure of the showmen. I have the greatest respect for them. They took this ride and all the fairs round in any weather, and it's often forgotten that all the stuff in the museum once belonged to them, and originated with them. They are a real community, and the switchback couldn't have been made without them.

You only have to look in the pages of *The World's Fair* to see how strong the family feeling is. In the modern world it often seems that relatives and family connections are abandoned to the city, but the weddings and funerals on a fairground bring hundreds or sometimes thousands of people together, whether or not they can afford to be there. Scan the obituary pages of *The World's Fair* and you'll see people remembered on the anniversary of their death from years ago. I know that many would find that and some of the poetry printed there sentimental, but I don't, because Nottingham Goose Fair, Hull Fair, King's Lynn Mart, or your local fair wouldn't be there without them, and I know very well that my switchback wouldn't have even been thought of if it hadn't been for the people who get the fairs about the country.

APPENDIX

THE THURSFORD COLLECTION

STEAM ENGINES

The following are all fully restored.

Burrell

King Edward VII	Built 1905. No 2780. An 8hp showman's engine, rebuilt as a full scenic engine in 1919–20.
Alexandra	Built 1908. No 3075. An 8hp showman's engine.
Victory	Built 1919–20. No 3827. An 8hp showman's engine. Built as a scenic engine from new.

A Burrell general purpose engine. Built 1926. No 4045. 5hp.

Fearless	A general purpose engine. Built 1927. No 4081. 7hp single cylinder. This is thought to be the last engine made by Burrells at Thetford.

Aveling & Porter

An Aveling & Porter light locomotive. Built 1928. No 12186. 5hp.
An Aveling & Porter traction engine. Built 1923–4. No 10487. 6hp. This engine could be converted to a steam roller.
An Aveling & Porter steam ploughing engine. Built 1917. No 8890. 14hp.

Ruston & Proctor

A Ruston & Proctor general purpose engine. Built 1910. No 39872. 7hp.

Garrett

Medina	A showman's engine. Built 1920. No 33902. 4hp.

Clayton

A Clayton steam wagon. Built 1927–8. No 1136. 3-way tipping body.

Foden

A Foden chain drive overtype tractor. Type D. Built 1928–9. No 13358.

There are two stationary steam engines, a Marshall of 1890 and a Tilghman of 1890, and a stationary diesel engine built in the 1930s by the Manchester firm of Crossley. Also on view is the very beautiful centre engine built for a roundabout in 1889 by Frederick Savage. There are 24 barn or oil engines by all the leading manufacturers, and 30 other large traction engines and showman's engines, including *Unity*, the fourth of the Thurston engines, which is undergoing restoration at the time of writing. Outside the main building is the railway engine *Cackler*; built by Hudswell Clerk in 1889, it runs on a 2ft gauge set of rails and now gives a tour of the gardens. Among other items to be seen is a large threshing machine and several wagons, including John Thurston's living wagon.

ORGANS

There are nine large dance or fairground organs by most of the leading manufacturers, including Gavioli, Marenghi, Carl Frei, Wellerhaus, Hooghuys, Mortier and Decap.

The WURLITZER is the fourth largest organ of its kind ever in Europe and was built in 1931–2 for the Paramount Theatre in Leeds. There are 1,339 pipes, measuring from ½in to 16ft in length in two complete rooms fronted by shutters. The 19 ranks give a corresponding 19 tone colours. This organ is a favourite of Reginald Dixon who says of it:

> During my career as a theatre, or as some say a cinema organist, I have played more instruments than I can possibly remember, pipe organs and electronic organs. I was introduced to some of the pipe organs when they were first installed in their original theatres. A number of these instruments have been transplanted with varying success. In my opinion the finest Wurlitzer in Britain today is the ex-Leeds Paramount organ now in the Cushing organ museum at Thursford. On May 20–1 1978 I was invited to give a concert on this instrument. I was so delighted with the sound, also the wonderful mechanical and electrical condition that I contacted my recording manager, Bob Barratt, and Stuart Eltham, the engineer at EMI. They carried out acoustic tests which resulted in my making two of my most successful LPs. I would like to add that I first played this Wurlitzer back in the early 'thirties when it was situated in the Paramount Theatre in Leeds and the sounds on this instrument gave me a number of ideas for the specification of my design for the new organ in the Tower Ballroom, Blackpool, back in 1934–5.

FAIRGROUND RIDE

The Gondola Switchback, built in 1896 by Frederick Savage, King's Lynn, Norfolk.

*   *   *   *   *

The museum is open every day from Easter weekend to 31 October, and every Sunday and Bank Holiday throughout the year from 2.00pm–5.30pm. There are live concerts on the Wurlitzer every Tuesday evening at 8.00pm from June to the end of September, and live musical shows each day. The nearest railway station is King's Lynn or Norwich.